Weeding Library Collections — II

WEEDING LIBRARY COLLECTIONS – II

_____ *Second Revised Edition* _____

STANLEY J. SLOTE

LIBRARIES UNLIMITED, INC.
Littleton, Colorado
1982

LIBRARIES UNLIMITED, INC.
P.O. Box 263
Littleton, Colorado 80160

Library of Congress Cataloging in Publication Data

Slote, Stanley J.
    Weeding library collections--II.

    Bibliography: p. 187
    Includes index.
    1. Discarding of books, periodicals, etc.
I. Title.
Z703.6.S55 1982   025.2'16   81-20724
ISBN 0-87287-283-1   AACR2

Libraries Unlimited books are bound with Type II nonwoven material that meets
and exceeds National Association of State Textbook Administrators' Type II
nonwoven material specifications Class A through E.

This book is dedicated to Marie G. Merskey, who bravely permitted me to apply my theoretical findings to her outstanding public library in Harrison, New York. It was this cooperation which ultimately helped hundreds of other librarians to apply a tested and proven technique to their own collections.

TABLE OF CONTENTS

PART 1
Background and Introduction to Weeding

PART 2
The Weeding Process

_11_

This book is based upon several research projects undertaken over a period of 18 years, field experience in weeding all or parts of some 20 libraries throughout the United States and Canada, and day-long workshop/seminars on weeding that I have presented 30 times, from Regina, Saskatchewan to Baton Rouge, Louisiana. The most frequent question asked at these workshops was whether I had a detailed, step-by-step explanation of how to weed a library.

Part 1, whose source is the first edition of *Weeding Library Collections*, deals with the broad background of weeding and weeding practice. It also establishes the research basis for Part 2, which is a step-by-step explanation of all of the preferred methods of weeding. Both parts are applicable to all kinds of materials in all kinds of libraries. Part 2 is completely new, and includes forms and techniques which have appeared nowhere else. For those readers who want to weed and don't want to be burdened with theory and background, I suggest starting with Part 2.

This work has been designed to be used for four distinct purposes:

1. As a comprehensive source summarizing the opinion, knowledge, and serious research in the field of weeding.

2. As a do-it-yourself guide for librarians wishing to weed out their present collections. It is the aim of this book not only to explain and justify its methods, but to include a step-by-step procedure for "weeding without tears."

3. As a textbook in library schools, especially in courses that deal with the acquisition and maintenance of library collections, for weeding is one of the best techniques available for the long-range building of useful collections.

4. As a stimulus to further study in this entire area. It is hoped that libraries using the recommended methods will measure and report upon the costs of weeding and the impact of such weeding upon changes in the amount of circulation and in user satisfaction.

The two parts of the collection that can be identified with confidence are the "core collection" (which will satisfy 95 to 99 percent of the demands upon the present collection) and a "weedable" part (which represents very little use-potential — 1 to 5 percent). It might be helpful to think in terms of "positive selection" (the volumes to be retained in the core) and "negative selection" (the volumes to be weeded). Thus, the term "weedable" is used as an antonym for "core collection."

It is not suggested that the "weedable" part of the collection be destroyed, thrown out, or even removed from the library. There is sympathy, but not agreement, with Carter Davidson, who suggested that libraries "burn, bury, sell or give away the rest [i.e., the weeded collection]."[1] No judgment is made other than to identify this part of the collection as having little practical use. The author is not out to destroy society's literary heritage. On the contrary, he feels strongly that ideally *any* book should be made readily available to *everyone*, as *rapidly* and *painlessly* as possible. Thus, secondary storage, centralized regional collections, and other subordinate means of preservation are implied. Nevertheless, the author feels strongly that the weeded volumes should be segregated and removed from the open stacks or primary areas which house the regular circulating collection.

While this book is based partially upon a doctoral dissertation, to which frequent reference will be made (the *Five Libraries Study*), an attempt has been made to exclude the more obscure and complex aspects of the original dissertation. Readers interested in the statistical evidence and the detailed methodology of the original project are advised to read the original work.[2] Nevertheless, the conclusions of the present work have been based upon controlled study, statistical verification, and several field studies. Its concepts have been applied and verified.

The study of the serious literature in weeding is an essential part of this report. The literature tended to validate the author's findings and to indicate the applicability of the methods and techniques to other types of collections, especially university and college collections. It is for this reason that the more serious works are covered in some detail.

Stanley J. Slote

REFERENCES

1. Carter Davidson, "The Future of the College Library," *College and Research Libraries* IV (March 1943), pp. 115-16.

2. Stanley James Slote, "The Predictive Value of Past-Use Patterns of Adult Fiction in Public Libraries for Identifying Core Collections" (unpublished Ph.D. dissertation, Rutgers University, 1970). University Microfilms, Inc., Ann Arbor, MI, No. 71-3104.

ACKNOWLEDGMENTS

Special thanks are due to the following people, who assisted me with the research necessary to produce this book: Marie G. Merskey, Judith Conway, Bette Gorton, Lois Witt, Honora Dougherty, Professors Ralph Blasingame, Thomas Mott, Ernest R. DeProspo, Neal Harlow, Joseph Naus, and Philip Clark. Much assistance was received from James E. Bryant, William Urban, Veronica Carey, Marian Gerhardt, Bettie Diver, Audrey Tirendi, Barbara Hull, Carol L. Ginsburg, Ronnie E. Teich, Juliette Levinton, Miriam Guido, and Salvatore M. Addotta. Mary F. Tomaselli edited the entire work, made a number of valuable suggestions, and is the author of the index.

"What are countless books to me,
and libraries of which the owner
in his whole life will scarcely read
the titles?"
—Seneca 4 B.C.-65 A.D.

"If you want roome for modern
books, it is easy to remove
the less useful into a more
remote place."
—Thomas Hollis, 1725
(quoted by Urquhart)

PART 1

Background and Introduction to Weeding

1

BACKGROUND TO WEEDING

INTRODUCTION

It has long been an expressed standard of libraries to weed collections on a regular basis. For instance, the *Proposed Standards for Adult Services in Public Libraries in New York State*, 1969, states:

Withdrawal

Much of the material in the community library is expendable within ten years.[1]

Annual withdrawals ... should average at least five percent of the total collection.[2]

These typical statements are only two of dozens of such statements that can be found; they consistently recommend the removal of books from the collection. Even more specific advice can be found in the ALA pamphlet, *Weeding the Small Library Collection*.[3] Here a six-page detailed paper has been issued to encourage library weeding. It is a "why, when, who, and how" pamphlet which advises librarians to "take courage and weed." In addition, leading practitioners of librarianship have called for continuous and aggressive weeding of collections. Carter and Bonk call for weeding to be a "regular, continuing, and steady process."[4] McGaw says that it improves the "efficiency and vitality of a collection."[5] Anderson points out that unnecessary items weaken a library.[6] Over the years librarians have been barraged by an almost endless stream of advice of this sort.

In spite of the advice, it has been observed and reported that too little weeding is being practiced and that library shelves contain quantities of unused and unwanted materials. It is hard to find practicing librarians who feel that sufficient weeding is being done in their libraries.

REASONS FOR WEEDING

In the face of rapidly growing collections, shortage of space, and the high cost of storing books on open stacks, there are rather potent reasons for vigorous weeding. It has been reported that Yale can store "four and one-half times as many books ... by the Yale Compact Storage Plan as in conventional stack arrangement."[7] This use of compact storage for less-used materials should not be overlooked, especially in the face of growing resistance to budget increases for new construction now being experienced in *all* types of libraries.

It should be noted that an increase in stack space is often the immediate cause of a much larger construction program. The real impact of expanding collections beyond their present library capacity must be related to the proper balance and functioning of the entire library. If one assumes that in the designing of new libraries an idealized relationship between book and non-book space is achieved, then the addition of new books beyond the original capacity of a building has some very expensive implications. In 1980, *Library Journal* indicated that 90 new public library buildings had an average cost of $58.07 per square foot,[8] or about $16.59 per volume of designed book capacity. (On an average, the architects designed new buildings to contain 3½ volumes per square foot of enclosed floor area.) Therefore, libraries considering the expansion of their collections could well consider this additional cost as the probable long-range result of such expansion.

Two related aspects of these costs might be considered. In 1980, for instance, the costs of building new academic libraries ranged from $6.60 per volume capacity to $57.14 per volume.[9] This seems to indicate that a wide range of factors are involved, and that a new library may find itself spending considerably more or less than $16.59 per volume for expansion. This observation calls for more study and analysis, with the goal of creating greater efficiency in the design of new facilities. However, the $16.59 figure must be considered only a point of departure when one considers the cost of expansion.

The other aspect, rarely mentioned in the literature, is that the actual space taken up by books is a small part of a new library building. Fremont Rider mentioned that only 10 percent of the cubic area taken up by book stacks contains books.[10] In 1980, *Library Journal* reported that academic libraries were built having a book capacity between 1.23 and 5.12 volumes per square foot of enclosed space.[11] This means that at full capacity a library actually used about 1/40th, or 2½ percent, of its enclosed area for books.[12] Thus it seems reasonable, when thinking of expanding collections, to think in terms of the true needs: on an average every book added over the designed capacity of a library should ultimately require building expansion equal to 40 times the amount of space taken up by the actual book itself.

While compact storage is less expensive than open stack storage, other suggestions to solve the over-all space problem should not be overlooked. One of the most obvious is to substitute some type of microfilm for the usual hard-covered book. Unfortunately, until greater user acceptance is gained, it is likely that such a solution would reduce usage considerably and at the same time increase service costs.

FACTORS DISCOURAGING WEEDING

In view of the pressing space problems, it is difficult to understand why more weeding has not been undertaken. A number of factors have discouraged weeding.

Emphasis on numbers. The number of books in a library is often considered a criterion of the quality of a library. Thus librarians, playing the numbers game, may tend to keep obsolete books to be included in the official book count. While many librarians reject the validity of a number count as a sensible quality measure, the official reporting forms for years emphasized book counts in the data to be submitted to higher authorities.

Professional work pressures. Weeding has generally been considered a professional task. In many instances, work pressures have not left librarians much time to perform the tasks of weeding. When it is considered that not only must weeding decisions be made, but that the card catalog, shelf list, and other records be maintained, the tasks and the time required to do them become intimidating to understaffed libraries.

Sacredness of collection. There are emotional and intellectual blocks against removing books from a collection. Many people consider books to be valuable records of human heritage and therefore almost sacred. The removal of any book becomes painful. Such indiscriminate retention of books does not serve the public. Books that are not being used but that have historical value belong in a depository. A public library that is *serving* the public needs to have a collection that is up to date and changing.

Collections will change, however, in spite of efforts to keep them intact. What is available to the reader is *not* what has been so carefully selected and purchased. Access to the reader is reduced by:

1. Theft and vandalism. Collections do not consist of all the books which have been purchased. Losses due to theft and vandalism will change a collection. Collections are routinely weeded of the newest and most wanted volumes, by the patrons themselves. Thus the original collection, which was carefully selected, is not the collection that remains on the library's shelves.

2. Misshelved books. A misshelved book generally no longer exists for the readers. They are unlikely to have access to it either through the card catalog or through normal browsing in subject areas—two basic access points to a collection. Unless shelf-reading is constant, regular, and careful, a part of the collection has disappeared (for all practical purposes) just as surely as if the books had been stolen. Furthermore, especially in academic libraries, intentional misshelving is a common technique that a patron uses to assure temporary but easy access to a particular book. If this practice is not prevented, the working collection is considerably different from the collection originally acquired.

3. Circulation. Circulating collections are not intact since substantial segments are in the hands of the clients. It is not uncommon to have a fourth of a collection circulating at any given time. Of the volumes that are circulating, most will eventually be returned, but there are a certain number of books which, by virtue of being much wanted, will almost always be out. Faculty loans in college and university libraries often are non-recallable and therefore not part of the readily usable collection. As far as users are concerned, they are not dealing with the collection as originally established, but with a collection that is on the shelves at the moment they are in the library. Therefore, it is inconsistent to maintain that the collection acquired is identical to the collection available. An attack on weeding cannot be based on the concept of keeping the integrity, unity, and overall design of the collection. Such unity has already been destroyed.

Conflicting criteria. Hard-to-apply and sometimes conflicting criteria have often made weeding an arduous and disturbing task. Weeders are torn between keeping the books people want and the "good" books. Librarians want balance, wide subject coverage, and quality. An attempt was made to apply these criteria when the volumes originally were selected. Then the weeder, frequently the person who selected the book in the first place, must make a subjective decision to discard a book previously judged worthy. This makes for difficult decision-making.

The weeding process is not without its risks. How many librarians have wished they had saved old telephone directories, mail-order catalogs, local newspapers, and a wide range of other items now sought after? Katz points out that the vast majority of nineteenth-century local newspapers were completely destroyed, with, at best, only given issues saved.[13] As anyone who has ever cleaned out an attic or basement knows, only a few days pass before a use is found for something just irretrievably discarded. In libraries, this risk must be minimized by some centralized responsibility for the collection of less-used materials.

While this study is unable to overcome the resistance caused by all of the above factors, it has aimed at making the physical and intellectual processes of weeding much simpler. If *objective* weeding criteria are used, weeding decisions are easier to make. Even clerical personnel, presumably more available than professionals, can be utilized for this work. With more certainty in weeding decisions, more extensive weeding could be done.

SUMMARY

It seems extremely timely that more attention be focused on weeding. Librarians are faced with economic pressures and demands for accountability for their expenditures. If ever there were a time for innovation in library services, attitudes, and operations, it is now. If, by realistic thinning of collections, librarians can reduce their requests for increased capital costs and at the same time increase the services being rendered, they will be answering the challenge in a way most acceptable to society.

REFERENCES

1. New York Library Association, Standards Committee and Subcommittees of the Adult Services Section, *Proposed Standards for Adult Services in Public Libraries in New York State* (New York: Library Association, March 1969), p. 7.

2. Ibid., p. 8.

3. American Library Association, Small Libraries Project, *Weeding the Small Library Collection.* Supplement A to Small Libraries Project Pamphlet No. 5 (Chicago: American Library Association, 1962).

4. Mary Duncan Carter and Wallace John Bonk, *Building Library Collections* (3rd ed. Metuchen, NJ): Scarecrow Press, 1969), p. 138.

5. Howard F. McGaw, "Policies and Practices in Discarding," *Library Trends* IV (January 1956), p. 277.

6. Polly G. Anderson, "First Aids for the Ailing Adult Book Collection," *Bookmark* XXI (November 1961), p. 47.

7. Lee Ash, *Yale's Selective Book Retirement Program* (Hamden, CT: Archon Books, 1963), p. 52.

8.   *Library Journal* CV (December 1, 1980), p. 2477.

9.   *Library Journal* CV (December 1, 1980), pp. 2465-77.

10.   Fremont Rider, *Compact Book Storage* (New York: Hadham Press, 1949), p. 8.

11.   Barbara Livingston, "Academic Library Building in 1980," *Library Journal* CV (December 1, 1980), pp. 2465-66.

12.   The computation for arriving at this figure uses 6x9 inches as the size of the average volume, a figure reported by Kilpatrick and Van Hoesen as the size of the median volume in their study, "The Heights of Three Hundred and Fifty Thousand Volumes," which appeared in the July 1935 issue of *Library Quarterly.* By sampling a number of volumes, we estimate the average width of a volume to be 1⅔ inches. This means that the average volume contains 90 cubic inches. Figuring the average library to have 8-foot ceilings, and therefore 8 cubic feet of volume per square foot of floor space, and using the 3½ books per square foot as reported above, we find that the average new library has 7/16th of a book (or 41 cubic inches) per cubic foot of enclosed area. This works out to about 2½ percent of the 1,728 cubic inches in a cubic foot.

13.   William A. Katz, *Introduction to Reference Work, Vol. II: Reference Services* (New York: McGraw-Hill, 1969), p. 87.

2

CONVENTIONAL GUIDELINES TO WEEDING

While many authorities have recommended weeding, it should be emphasized that opinions on weeding have not been unanimous. Some have suggested either no weeding or weeding with great limitations. In addition, even those recommending it have stated a diversity of goals for this activity. Much of this diversity of opinion reflects the philosophies, concepts, attitudes, and prejudices of the writers. More often, the opinions are the results of practical problems facing administrators of ever-growing collections. The concept follows the need. Finally, there have been opinions based upon the needs of specific research projects, where assumptions are forced upon researchers if their studies are to have some broad-based foundation. All these influences can be seen in the following goals:

That all collections should be kept absolutely intact. Books represent the accumulated recorded written heritage of civilization; therefore, wherever they may be, they should be preserved. This is the position of the anti-weeder. The removal of anything is considered profane. Typical of this attitude is an article by John Neufeld, entitled "S-O-B Save Our Books." The term "s.o.b." pretty much sums up his reaction toward anyone attempting to remove any book from a collection.[1]

That collections may be weeded, gingerly, by professionals only, using good judgment, not rules. Only the experienced and trained librarian can perform this task. However, general guidelines for weeding can be established. The goal is to maintain a well-balanced collection that will match the needs and the wants of users, real and potential. Libraries attached to other institutions (schools, universities, or businesses) should have a further review of the books recommended for weeding, to be performed by members of the main institution (teachers, professors, researchers). Otherwise, "good" books or "useful" ones are likely to be removed.

This position probably represents the majority opinion in the country today. It has been reinforced by unpleasant experiences when weeding has been handled by non-librarians. It has been generated by the alienation of members of faculties, for example, when weeding has occurred without their being consulted. In part, this position has been taught in library schools and represents an honest belief of some of the leaders in the profession. Typical of this attitude is that of Bedsole, who insists that "sound professional judgment of any specific work will always be required."[2]

Even people who have strongly suggested other methods, which they have validated by rigidly disciplined research, are hesitant to offend professionalism. Fussler, who has done some of the most fruitful investigation in the field of weeding, felt forced to defend himself in the face of rather severe criticism from the faculty:

> Furthermore there is little question that the overall effectiveness of any formula for selecting books for storage [weeding] would be improved considerably if one or more scholars reviewed the titles recommended for storage.[3]

This conclusion is *not* supported by any research evidence in his studies, and in fact might be in direct *conflict* with his findings.

That collections should be so weeded that they are maintained at a predetermined physical size. This aim, popular with some administrators, is an attempt to relieve the pressure for new construction caused by the ever-growing collections.

This approach is taken by Silver in a term paper prepared for an operations research course at the Massachusetts Institute of Technology (M.I.T.):

> One serious problem now confronting the librarians is that the extra shelf space is rapidly diminishing due to the acquisition of new books. A possible course of action to remedy the situation is the use of weeding.[4]

Silver feels that it would be useful to librarians to find a way to keep constant the number of volumes in a collection.

This approach, as with all the others, is not without its critics. Rider implies that such stabilization of the size of a collection is not feasible. He maintains that as human knowledge grows, so must libraries. Just in one area, reference, the number of books gets larger each year. No college has succeeded in stabilizing collections. The continuations of periodicals, government documents, society transactions, etc., prevent stabilization.[5]

That library stacks should be stocked with those volumes likely to give the library the greatest circulation. This objective highlights the need for getting maximum usage out of social institutions and their resources. It also points up the conflict between two schools of librarianship: those who wish to give the user what he *wants*; and those who wish to give him what he *needs* (or what is "good" for him).

NEWER GUIDELINES TO WEEDING

That weeding should increase circulation. One must search thoroughly in order to find support for weeding to maximize use; it sounds unprofessional and therefore is best approached more indirectly. Gans states that "a library that is not used sufficiently is a waste of resources, ... the library must be user-oriented."[6] More to the point is a study by Ruth Polson. She reports an 81 percent increase in circulation, "despite a decrease of more than one-third in the book stock," after weeding. The tone of her report implies that weeding is a tool for circulation increase.[7]

That collections should be weeded so that the speed of access is increased and so that the accuracy in retrieval is improved. It has been observed, mainly in special libraries, that small, compact collections of materials reduce the time needed for retrieval.[8] In libraries where speed is essential, this is often a prime consideration. For instance, in newspaper libraries (morgues) where deadlines must be met, the growth of collections and cumulation of irrelevant materials can block reasonable usage.

That those books least likely to be used in the future be removed. In contrast with the goals of maintaining collections at a given size, this approach attempts to keep a collection that will satisfy a predetermined amount of future use. It tries to identify core collections that will satisfy 95 percent or 99 percent of the present demands made upon the collection, and to do this with the smallest identifiable core collection. A very large part of the serious research in weeding has used this approach. As Fussler and Simon state:

> The major purpose of the study was to answer this question: Will any kind of statistical procedure predict with reasonable accuracy the frequencies with which groups of books with defined characteristics are likely to be used in a research library.[9]

One characteristic of these studies is the implication that weeded books be removed to secondary storage in less accessible areas. Another recurring theme relates to the endless growth of the size of collections and the constant pressure for new buildings. The studies often attempt to determine long-range solutions and frequently try to make predictions of the percentages of the collection that can be removed at various levels of retained usage. They accept, as a basic premise, that usage is a valid criterion for keeping volumes on open stacks, or in main library buildings. Furthermore, they aim to find objective criteria for weeding. This present volume has accepted these assumptions as being basic to its theme.

ADDITIONAL METHODS

While all of the above reflect some current goals of weeding, other methods of reaching these same goals have been suggested. It is obvious, for instance, that the space needed to store materials can be reduced substantially through the use of micro-reproduction. Microfilm, microfiche, and microprint can be found in libraries. While many people feel that such reduction in size makes the materials harder to use, the whole question of size reduction is an important but unresolved one.

In addition, libraries have attacked the problems through limiting the subject areas of their collections or assigning different specializations to other libraries in a cooperative fashion. The Library of Congress has agreed with the National Library of Medicine and the Department of Agriculture Library not to overlap their specialized collections unnecessarily. The Farmington Plan, now defunct, was another attempt to assign areas of subject or language specialization.

Many other attempts have been made. Union catalogs, interlibrary loans, deposit collections, and library systems have all contributed in some way toward fulfilling the above goals.

REFERENCES

1.   John Neufeld, "S-O-B Save Our Books," *RQ* VI (Fall 1966), pp. 25-28.

2.   Danny T. Bedsole, "Formulating a Weeding Policy for Books in a Special Library," *Special Libraries* XLIX (May-June 1958), p. 207.

3.   Herman H. Fussler and Julian L. Simon, *Patterns in the Use of Books in Large Research Libraries* (Chicago: University of Chicago Press, 1969), p. 144.

4.   Edward A. Silver, "A Quantitative Appraisal of the M.I.T. Science Library Mezzanine with an Application to the Problem of Limited Shelf Space" (unpublished term paper for M.I.T. graduate course 8:75, Operations Research, 1962), p. 2.

5.   Fremont Rider, *The Scholar and the Future of the Research Library* (New York: Hadham Press, 1944), pp. 44-46.

6.   Herbert J. Gans, "The Public Library in Perspective," in *The Public Library and the City*, ed. by Ralph W. Conant (Cambridge, MA: M.I.T. Press, 1965), p. 69.

7.   Ruth E. Polson, "When Your Library Joins a System, What Can You Expect?" *Illinois Libraries* XLIX (January 1967), pp. 26-38.

8.   Stanley J. Slote, "An Approach to Weeding Criteria for Newspaper Libraries," *American Documentation* XIX (April 1968), p. 168.

9.   Fussler and Simon, *Patterns in the Use of Books in Large Research Libraries*, p. 5.

3

LIBRARY STANDARDS RELATING
TO WEEDING

A study of the various standards will show that weeding is either recommended or completely disregarded; it is never suggested that no weeding be done. If recommended, however, the force with which weeding is emphasized varies considerably. These standards range from 1) no weeding, to 2) minimal weeding, to 3) rather forthright statements quantifying the process. Listed in this chapter are some examples of standards in the order of their emphasis. No attempt has been made to be all-inclusive. Accreditation standards, state and local standards, and standards found in textbooks have been omitted. The statements below are generally national standards formulated or accepted by a national library or an educational or governmental organization.

In general, the types of standards relating to weeding may be divided into five classifications.

STANDARDS NOT MENTIONING WEEDING

The 1969 *Standards for School Media Programs*[1] and "Guidelines for Establishing Junior College Libraries," 1963,[2] make no mention of weeding at all. These standards generally are concerned with promoting the establishment or recognition of relatively new kinds of libraries. Apparently, it is hard to think in terms of weeding a library which has not yet come into existence, or which has only recently been established.

STANDARDS THAT HINT AT WEEDING

Some standards just hint at a need for weeding. The *Standards for Children's Services in Public Libraries*, for example, handle weeding almost parenthetically:

Continuous critical evaluation of children's materials throughout the development of the collection — in initial selection, replacement, duplication, and *withdrawal* [italic mine] — is essential to maintain the effectiveness and quality of resources.[3]

Even less forceful is the approach found in "Objectives and Standards for Special Libraries." Here the writer tries to report what actually is happening in practice, rather than what should happen.

THE SIZE OF A SPECIAL LIBRARY COLLECTION DEPENDS UPON THE AMOUNT OF MATERIAL AVAILABLE THAT IS PERTINENT TO THE ORGANIZATION'S SPECIAL NEEDS.

The purpose and use of the special library's collection influence its size. Some libraries need large reference collections, multiple copies, and works that have historical value; others have highly selective collections, keep currently useful literature only, and retain only in microform older periodical sets and items of decreasing usefulness. *Many libraries discard little used materials if they are available in the area.* [Italics mine.) The rate and direction of growth of the library's collection should reflect the continuing requirements of the library's clientele.[4]

Another approach focuses on replacement: discarding is recommended only when new editions are acquired. *Recommended Standards for Libraries in Hospitals* uses this approach:

Out-of-date editions must be replaced by the most recent as soon as possible, and discarded from stock. An outdated book is a trap for the unwary student.[5]

STANDARDS RECOMMENDING WEEDING

The third case of standards specifically recommends weeding, occasionally identifies what is to be weeded, but does not tell how often, how much, or even how. For example, the *Standards for Library Services in Health Care Institutions* says:

Regular replacement of worn-out and outdated library materials should be planned and budgeted annually.[6]

Selection of materials should be based on an established written policy.... This policy should cover scope of subject matter, retention periods, acceptance of gifts, and criteria for weeding and discarding.[7]

Somewhat more specific, but still rather limited, are the standards in the ALA "Standards for College Libraries":

Obsolete materials, such as outmoded books, superseded editions, incomplete sets of longer works, broken files of unindexed journals, superfluous duplicates, and worn out or badly marked volumes, should be continuously weeded, with the advice of faculty members concerned.[8]

In line with this type of recommendation are the following three standards published in 1964 by the Department of Health, Education, and Welfare:

1. *Recommended Standards for Junior High School Libraries*
   The collection should be kept up-to-date and in good condition by continuous discarding, binding, and addition of new titles.[9]

2. *Recommended Standards for Senior High School Libraries*
   Provision should be made through an adequate budget for the continuous process of replacement of out-of-date titles with new editions, of worn copies with fresh ones, of obsolete titles with current ones.

   There should be regular replacement of encyclopedias by the purchase of one new set of the latest edition every other year....[10]

In this last recommendation there is the first glimmer of specific instruction in the specifics of weeding:

3. *Recommended Standards for Junior College Libraries*
   This standard calls for "systematic and regular discarding of obsolete materials."[11]

Young Adult Services in the Public Library provides more emphatic recommendation of weeding, but weeding criteria are vague:

> The young adult collection should be drastically weeded to keep it alive, fresh, and attractive. Titles that are not read with interest should be discarded. Care, however, should be taken not to discard unusual and special titles which need to be introduced by the librarian to the young adult to show their true values. In the field of sports, vocational titles, and junior novels, where there is a plethora of titles, it is advisable to limit rebinding and replacement to the most useful and outstanding books, and to use available funds to purchase new titles to round out the collection.[12]

The older *School Library Standards*, now superseded by *Standards for School Library Programs*, also recommends weeding in general terms:

> The collections are continuously re-evaluated in relation to changing curriculum content, new instructional methods, and current needs of teachers and students. Appropriate materials are obtained for these new developments. This process of re-evaluation also leads to the replacement of outmoded materials with those that are up-to-date, the discarding of materials no longer useful, and the replacement of materials in poor repair.[13]

> It is assumed that certain factors tend to operate to keep sufficient balance between materials acquired and those discarded, so that the materials collections, particularly in very large schools, do not become disproportionately large.[14]

This latter assumption is rather questionable when compared to the observable facts.

STANDARDS ESTABLISHING QUANTITIES

The fourth class of standards not only specifically requires weeding, but makes some attempt to establish weeding criteria and to define the amount of weeding that is advisable. *Public Library Service* (1956) not only explains that currently *useful* books are dead after 10 years but advises a reduction in the collection at the average rate of 5 percent through weeding:

> Systematic removal from collections of materials no longer useful is essential to maintaining the purposes and quality of resources.

> Unnecessary items remaining in a collection can weaken a library as surely as insufficient acquisitions. In time such material characterizes the whole collection, over-shadowing newer and more useful purchases. Outdated material should obviously be removed; discredited material deserves the same action, although this requires more judgment; and items no longer of interest should give way in the process so appropriately termed "weeding." With few exceptions, public libraries are not centers for historical research, except in the field of local history when not adequately supplied elsewhere in the community. They do not need to retain material for a possible future scholar, and their day-to-day effectiveness for regular users decreases as they keep seldom-used material. The currently useful books which form the bulk of material in a public library collection are expendable or "dead" within ten years.

> Annual withdrawals from the collection should average at least 5 percent of the total collection.[15]

In 1962, the *Interim Standards for Small Public Libraries* accepted most of the above standards, some of them verbatim; but the *Interim Standards* highlighted the need for preserving some of the weeded material in larger centers:

> SYSTEMATIC REMOVAL FROM THE LIBRARY OF MATERIALS NO LONGER USEFUL IS ESSENTIAL TO MAINTAIN THE PURPOSE AND QUALITY OF THE COLLECTION.

> 1. Outdated and shabby material should obviously be removed; discredited material deserves the same action, although this requires more judgment; and items no longer of interest should be weeded out.

> 2. Material not actively used in small libraries but still occasionally needed should be withdrawn from the collection and sent to an authorized library center from which it can be borrowed for future use.

> 3. Annual withdrawals from the basic collection should average 5 percent of the total collection. In community libraries where much of the material is in a changing collection, this percentage may be lower.[16]

In 1967, the *Minimum Standards for Public Library Systems* again retained verbatim substantial sections of both the 1956 and 1962 standards but expanded upon them. While both quantitative and qualitative, they inject a note of uncertainty that has characterized weeding efforts in libraries. The entire section is quoted since it is interesting to note the specific word changes and to speculate on the attitudes that may have caused such changes. (Basic changes in content have been italicized.)

SYSTEMATIC REMOVAL OF MATERIALS NO LONGER USEFUL IS ESSENTIAL TO MAINTAINING THE PURPOSES AND QUALITY OF *RESOURCES*

Outdated, *seldom-used*, or shabby *items* remaining in the collection can weaken a library as surely as insufficient acquisitions. In time such material characterizes the whole collection, overshadowing newer and more useful purchases. Outdated materials should obviously be removed. With few exceptions, community libraries are not centers for historical research, except in the field of local history. Except for materials of special quality smaller community libraries do not ordinarily need to retain seldom-used items, for to do so may decrease day-to-day effectiveness. Larger community libraries whose *staff and building are adequate for proper maintenance of a more vaired collection* may be more generous in retention of seldom-used items.

   i. Annual withdrawals from community library collections should average at least 5 percent of the total collection. The community library collection should consist of currently useful materials. The bulk of material in the smaller community library is expendable or "dead" within ten years.

   ii. Headquarters libraries, reservoirs of quality materials from which community libraries draw, should carefully consider withdrawals and not necessarily make them conform to numerical ratios.

   iii. *Withdrawals made at any level should be offered to the next higher echelon of resources before they are destroyed.*[17]

It can be seen from the changes that three new emphases have been made. First, there is a focus on seldom-used materials. Such a use-criterion for weeding can lead to a realistic solution of weeding problems. Second, the offering of resources to higher echelons centers on the need to have different depths for different kinds of collections. Finally, the need for a larger staff for proper collection maintenance is also highlighted. However, in these standards adequate staff justifies less weeding, while for most practicing librarians it would permit more weeding.

Another quantified example is mentioned in the now superseded *Standards for School Library Programs*:

Back issues of periodicals needed for reference work and for other purposes are retained in the school library for a time span covering at least five years.[18]

Note, however, that this approach tells how long an item is to be kept at a minimum and not when it is to be discarded.

RECOMMENDED STANDARDS

The author recommends a fifth version of standards for libraries. This would be a standard, including all of the following points, for material that normally circulates.

1. The objective of weeding would be to maintain a core collection of books that would satisfy 95 percent to 99 percent of the present demands made upon the entire present collection.

2. All books weeded would be considered for secondary or centralized storage.

3. One complete weeding of the library should take place in each year.

4. The weeding criterion to be used should be based solely upon the likelihood of a volume's being used in the future.

5. The shelf-time period established for each library should satisfy the above standards and should result in an objective similar to this: "All volumes should be removed that have not been circulated since (date)." This shelf-time period should take into account the use patterns of no less than one full year.

6. Similar criteria should be established and utilized, in modified form, for the different *types* of material as follows:
   a) For runs of periodicals, remove all before a specific publication date. This date should be established separately for each run.
   b) For reference books, weeding should be performed as for circulating works, attempting to keep a core representing 99 percent to 99.5 percent of the present usage.
   c) For archives and special works (such as works of local authors) no weeding should be done.

The basis for such standards will be developed in later chapters of this work. No such official standards exist at this time. However, some individual libraries are using the above standards, at least in part.

REFERENCES

1. American Association of School Librarians and the Department of Audiovisual Instruction of the National Education Association, *Standards for School Media Programs* (Chicago: American Library Association, 1969).

2. American Library Association, Association of College and Research Libraries, Committee on Standards, "Guidelines for Establishing Junior College Libraries," *College and Research Libraries* XXIV (November 1963), pp. 501-505.

3. American Library Association, Public Library Association, Subcommittee on Standards for Children's Service, *Standards for Children's Services in Public Libraries* (Chicago: American Library Association, 1964), p. 22.

4. Special Libraries Association, "Objectives and Standards for Special Libraries," *Special Libraries* LV (December 1964), p. 675.

5. Library Association, Hospital Libraries, *Recommended Standards for Libraries in Hospitals* (London: Library Association, 1965), p. 15.

6. American Library Association, Association of Hospital and Institution Libraries, *Standards for Library Services in Health Care Institutions* (Chicago: American Library Association, 1970), p. 13.

7. Ibid., p. 8.

8. American Library Association, Association of College and Research Libraries, Committee on Standards, "Standards for College Libraries," *College and Research Libraries* XX (July 1959), p. 277.

9. U.S. Department of Health, Education, and Welfare, *Survey of School Library Standards*, by Richard L. Darling, Circular No. 740, OE 15048 (Washington, DC: Government Printing Office, 1964), p. 42.

10. Ibid., p. 45.

11. Ibid., p. 48.

12. American Library Association, Public Library Association, Committee on Standards for Work with Young Adults in Public Libraries, *Young Adult Services in the Public Library* (Chicago: American Library Association, 1960), p. 27.

13. American Library Association, Association of School Librarians, *Standards for School Library Programs* (Chicago: American Library Association, 1960), p. 75.

14. Ibid., pp. 82-83.

15. American Library Association, Public Libraries Division, Coordinating Committee on Revision of Public Library Standards, *Public Library Service, A Guide to Evaluation, with Minimum Standards* (Chicago: American Library Association, 1956), pp. 34-35.

16. American Library Association, Public Library Association, Subcommittee on Standards for Small Libraries, *Interim Standards for Small Public Libraries: Guidelines toward Achieving the Goals of Public Library Service* (Chicago: American Library Association, 1963), p. 8.

17. American Library Association, Public Library Association, Standards Committee and Subcommittees, *Minimum Standards for Public Library Systems, 1966* (Chicago: American Library Association, 1967), pp. 39-40.

18. American Library Association, Association of School Librarians, *Standards for School Library Programs*, p. 79.

4

PRESENT WEEDING CRITERIA BASED ON JUDGMENT

DIFFICULTIES ENCOUNTERED IN SUBJECTIVE WEEDING

The mass of material. In the face of rather indecisive standards or goals for the weeding of libraries, there exists a wide range of specific advice on what to weed. Much of this advice assumes that librarians have the ability to make "good" weeding judgments, based upon their knowledge of the community of the users, of books in general, or their own collections, and of society's needs.

It is the contention of this writer that the above assumptions lack the validity usually assigned to them. For example, librarians are supposed to "know" books: to know what exists, what is worth acquiring, what the library holds, and what the library should hold. Can anyone really "know" about books? It is doubtful. The very mass of the accumulation seems to make it improbable. It is likely that there are between 45,000,000 and 50,000,000 different titles or works in the world.[1] The holdings of just a few of the major libraries seem to point to the validity of the estimate, although no definitive study has been made on the titles now in existence. Nevertheless, the British Museum contains 7,000,000 volumes, of which 75 percent are not among the 13,500,000 books held by the Library of Congress. Bibliothèque Nationale, with a strong emphasis on French works, contains 7,000,000 volumes. To this quantity, one must also consider the 400,000 new titles added internationally each year. In addition, the several hundred thousand government documents (restricted and unrestricted) published each year are generally not included in the 400,000 figure. To make the problem more complex, one might want to include the 1,000,000 serial titles, current and retrospective, and hundreds of thousands of other non-book items such as newspapers, phonograph records, pamphlets, films, film strips, and other forms collected by some libraries. The size of the stockpile creates an awesome problem for the librarian.

One of the ways librarians obtain information about books is through critical reviews. Unfortunately, only a small fraction of books published are reviewed. And even the reviews that do exist are a massive body of literature.

Another way to "know" books is to read them. A reasonably fast reader, with enough time (our average librarian?), might read one book a day. This would amount to 365 books per year or one-thousandth of the current output and perhaps one-hundred thousandth of the total of all works that exist. This does not even begin to deal with other serious problems that block this approach, such as one reader's inability to handle the diversity of languages, or the lack of availability of these volumes to librarians.

Can a librarian really "know" books? It is hard to believe that such knowledge can be anything but extremely perfunctory. It is hard even to "know" the literature in one restricted field like librarianship. There are at least 700 periodicals of librarianship. Counting regional periodicals, irregular ones, and newsletter types, the number must exceed 1,000. How many of these does the average librarian get to read? It is difficult to find anyone, even in the academic world, who feels that he keeps up with the literature of librarianship.

Knowledge of the community. Other assumptions upon which subjective weeding is based also have serious flaws. For example, librarians are charged with "knowing their communities" and thereby "catering to their needs." Is this possible? How many people even know their own needs and can cater to them? Or the needs and wants of their children? Their students? What unique characteristics, training, and experience do librarians have that equip them for such a commitment? If it is true that they understand and know how to serve their communities, why have they not done so?

Every survey of use shows that libraries get relatively little use. It has been estimated that only 10 percent of the adult population really use the public library[2] and that a large percentage of college students use their college library so rarely "that they would scarcely miss it if it ceased to exist."[3] Librarians have trouble satisfying the needs of their patrons, much less the community.

Consider the frequent failures that occur when the library tries to serve minority groups and the poor. No matter how exhaustive a study of a community is, there exists no agreed upon, specific, or valid response to the data. Do Spanish books substantially increase library usage by Puerto Ricans in New York? Do black studies and black subjects fill libraries with black readers? The answer to both questions, at least to now, is a qualified "no."

Therefore, the author tends to reject the purely professional and subjective approach to weeding. The assumption that librarians really "know" what books to retain to satisfy the patron is invalid, unless it is based upon *use studies* within a library. Furthermore, attempting to keep what is best for some vague non-user seems a waste, considering the difficulties encountered in trying to satisfy completely the present users. Why look for new challenges before responding to the older, closer, and more immediate challenge of running present libraries better?

In reading the following weeding criteria one must be suspicious of the basis of the judgments which created them. Nonetheless, these criteria do create a starting point for current weeding practice.

SPECIFIC WEEDING CRITERIA

The following weeding criteria has been culled from the sources in the special bibliography at the end of this chapter. Essentially this information has been published in the how-to literature of librarianship, usually for specific types of libraries. However, where the overlapping is great, no attempt has been made to identify the type of library involved. It is the purpose of this chapter to demonstrate the range of criteria available.

Weeding based upon appearance. The most universally accepted criterion for weeding is based upon the *appearance* of a volume. Often, however, this criterion calls for caution—to avoid discarding rare books—and for judgment—to determine whether or not the volume should be replaced. Some of the specific advice is to weed:

1. Books of antiquated appearance which might discourage use.
2. Badly bound volumes with soft pulpy paper and/or shoddy binding.
3. Badly printed works, including those with small print, dull or faded print, cramped margins, poor illustrations, paper that is translucent so that the print shows through.
4. Worn-out volumes whose pages are dirty, brittle, or yellow, with missing pages, frayed binding, broken backs, or dingy or dirty covers.

Weeding of superfluous or duplicate volumes. It is easier for most librarians to agree upon the criterion of weeding duplicate volumes than upon any other criterion, since this approach retains one copy of the title in the collection. Books similar to other books fall easily into this category. Some examples to weed are:

1. Unneeded duplicate titles.
2. Duplicates except for date or place or reprint.
3. Inexpensive reprints.
4. Older editions.
5. Editions in languages other than English when the English version is held by the library.
6. Highly specialized books when the library holds more extensive or more up-to-date volumes on the same subject.
7. Superfluous books on subjects of little interest to the local community.

Weeding based upon poor content. Weed:

1. When information is dated.
2. When book is poorly written.
3. When information is incorrect.
4. When improved editions exist.
5. Earlier titles in repetitious fiction series.

Weeding based upon language. Weed:

1. When the language is not called for in your library.
2. Editions in uncommon or foreign languages when edition in the native language is also held by the library.

Weeding based upon age alone. Frequently this advice is hedged by exception. Weed:

1. Books held 30 years or less.
2. Books over 20 years old.
3. If not in a standard list and over 10 years old.
4. Fiction best-sellers of ephemeral value after 10 years.
5. Out-of-date books and pamphlets.
6. Books over 5 years old.
7. Early volumes of serials.

Specific classes of books that particularly lend themselves to weeding. Weed:

1. Books that should not have been bought in the first place.
2. History books with inaccurate or unfair interpretations.
3. Grammars that are old.
4. Ordinary school dictionaries.
5. Almanacs and yearbooks that have been superseded.
6. Religion and philosophy: historical and explanatory texts when superseded; old theology; old commentaries on the Bible; sectarian literature; sermons; books on the conduct of life; popular self-help psychology.
7. In university collections:
    a) Inspirational literature, juveniles, elementary and secondary textbooks, non-contemporary minor authors, crank literature, biographies of obscure people.
    b) Personal war experiences.
    c) Student course outlines.
    d) Correspondence school material.
    e) Accession lists of general libraries.
    f) Press releases.
    g) Publications of colleges and universities: newspapers, newsletters, press releases, humor magazines, literature magazines edited by students; files of programs; non-current books of views, alumni publications.
    h) Programs of meetings.
    i) Speeches of officers of corporations published for purposes of advertising.
    j) Speeches of government officials.
    k) Dissertations.
    l) Subjects of little interest to a specific university because of its curriculum.
    m) Reprints.
    n) Mysteries.

Specific classes of works with specific age for weeding. Weed:

1. All ordinary textbooks after 10 years.
2. Books on medicine, inventions, radio, television, gardening, and business between 5 and 10 years old.
3. Travel books after 10 years.
4. Economics, science, and useful arts books in teachers' colleges, when the books are more than 10 years old.
5. Fiction best-sellers of ephemeral value after 10 years.
6. Senior encyclopedias from 5 to 10 years.
7. Encyclopedias at least every 10 years.
8. Encyclopedias at least every 5 years, preferably every year.
9. Junior encyclopedias from 3 to 5 years.
10. Almanacs, yearbooks and manuals—get the latest editions, and keep older editions at least 5, preferably 10 years.
11. Dictionaries—never.
12. Biographical sources—never.
13. Directories after 5 to 10 years but get the latest edition.
14. Inexpensive geographic sources—5 to 10 years. Expensive ones, never.
15. Social science, topical material, after 10 or 15 years.

Weeding criteria for periodicals and serials. Weed:

1. Periodicals not indexed.
2. Serials that have ceased publication and that have no cumulative index.
3. Incomplete sets.
4. Early volumes of serials, especially longer runs of 50 or 60 volumes.
5. Journals in English petroleum libraries after 13 years.

An example of specialized weeding criteria (a morgue or newspaper library). These criteria relate to cuts, which are engraved blocks used in the process of reproducing pictures in a newspaper.

1. Discard all cuts of women where the cuts are over 10 years old, and any cuts with out-of-date hairdos.
2. Discard all cuts of men, if middle-aged when picture was taken, where the cuts are over 15 years old.
3. Discard all cuts of men, if under 30 years old when pictures were taken, where the cuts are over 10 years old.
4. Discard mats when cuts exist.

5. Keep one good cut of ordinary people.

6. Keep three good cuts of better-known people.

7. Keep five good cuts of the famous.

8. Discard bad, blurry, useless cuts.

9. Discard duplicates.

10. Discard all cuts of school athletes 5 years after they stop playing, except those of great national stars. Keep them until death of star.

11. Discard cuts of all professional athletes 7 years after they stop playing, except those of big stars. Keep them until death of star.

12. Discard all cuts of the dead, except the famous. Keep these indefinitely.

13. Do not keep wedding, engagement, graduation cuts.

Hundreds of such sets of weeding criteria exist in the area of special librarianship, and this example (produced some years ago by this author) is typical of judgment weeding criteria.

Weeding criteria based upon use patterns. While this entire book relates to weeding criteria based upon previous use patterns, the suggested patterns are to be developed by carefully controlled statistical data. The use patterns below were developed, as were the other criteria in this chapter, by the judgment of experts. This is what accounts for the wide divergence of opinions. Weed:

1. Books not circulated in 3 years.

2. Books unused for 5 years that do not appear in a standard book list.

3. Books that have not circulated for 3 to 5 years, that have not been used for reference, and that are not standard titles.

4. If 5 years old and not circulated in the last year.

5. Books that have not been read in years.

6. Books not called for in a university library in 20 years.

Divergent opinion. It must be emphasized that there is a body of divergent opinion in the area of use patterns.

1. The fact that the volumes are not used in 1, 2, or 5 years is not proof that they are not needed.

2. The fact that a book has not circulated during the past few years should not be held to its discredit to an appreciable degree, since potential circulation value may still exist.

3. Discard one-column cuts in their ninth year, unless they have been re-used during this period, in which case they are to be weeded out in the fourteenth year.

Keeping criteria. A word might be added about "keeping" criteria, which are the other side of the coin of weeding criteria. If we know what to keep, we can weed the rest. Three examples of this kind of advice follow.

1. Keep if listed in one of the standard catalogs, such as *Standard Catalog for Public Libraries.*

2. Keep if charged out within the past 5 years.

3. If a title has been frequently used during the past few years, it should probably be retained.

SUMMARY OF WEEDING CRITERIA

Several characteristics of the above criteria might be noted.

1. In many cases, considerable work is needed to apply the criteria. The decision date may be impossible to reconstruct. For example, if the transaction card system is used, how does one tell when or how many times a volume has circulated? Or in another case, the checking of works against a standard catalog is a rather tedious job.

2. In many cases, the judgments to be made are based on vague, difficult interpretations. What is an "older edition," "small print," "superfluous books on a subject," etc.?

3. There are many contradictions among the criteria.

4. There is, nevertheless, some rationale to much of what is proposed. Many of these criteria seem to satisfy the needs for weeding criteria and might relate closely to more objective criteria produced by careful study.

REFERENCES

1. These figures represent an estimation by the author derived from information obtained from the Library of Congress.

2. Bernard Berelson, *The Library's Public* (New York: Columbia University Press, 1949), p. 10.

3. Harvie Branscomb, *Teaching with Books, A Study of College Libraries* (Chicago: Association of American Colleges and American Library Association, 1940), p. 39.

SPECIAL BIBLIOGRAPHY

The weeding criteria in this chapter are quoted from the following sources:

American Library Association. Small Libraries Project. *Weeding the Small Library Collection.* (Supplement A to Small Libraries Project Pamphlet No. 5.) Chicago: American Library Association, 1962.

Anderson, Polly G. "First Aids for the Ailing Adult Book Collection," *Bookmark* XXI (November 1961), pp. 47-49.

Ash, Lee. *Yale's Selective Book Retirement Program.* Hamden, CT: Archon Books, 1963.

Bedsole, Danny T. "Formulating a Weeding Policy for Books in a Special Library," *Special Libraries* XLIX (May-June 1958), pp. 205-209.

Boyer, Calvin J., and Nancy L. Eaton. *Book Selection Policies in American Libraries: An Anthology of Policies from College, Public and School Libraries.* Austin, TX: Armadillo Press, 1971.

Branscomb, Harvie. *Teaching with Books, A Study of College Libraries.* Chicago: Association of American Colleges and American Library Association, 1940.

Carter, Mary Duncan, and Wallace John Bonk. *Building Library Collections.* 3rd ed. Metuchen, NJ: Scarecrow Press, 1969.

Cole, P. F. "Journal Usage Versus Age of Journal," *Journal of Documentation* XIX (March 1963), pp. 1-11.

Currie, Dorothy H. *How to Organize a Children's Library.* Dobbs Ferry, NY: Oceana Publications, 1965.

Eliot, Charles W. "The Division of a Library into Books in Use, and Books Not in Use, with Different Storage Methods for the Two Classes of Books," *Library Journal* XXVII (July 1902), pp. 51-56.

Katz, William A. *Introduction to Reference Work, Vol. II: Reference Services.* New York: McGraw-Hill, 1969.

McGaw, Howard F. "Policies and Practices in Discarding," *Library Trends* IV (January 1956), pp. 269-82.

Mumford, L. Quincy. "Weeding Practices Vary," *Library Journal* LXXI (June 15, 1946), pp. 895-98.

Slote, Stanley J. "An Approach to Weeding Criteria for Newspaper Libraries," *American Documentation* XIX (April 1968), pp. 168-72.

U.S. Department of Health, Education, and Welfare. *Survey of School Library Standards*, by Richard L. Darling. Circular No. 740. OE 15048. Washington, DC: Government Printing Office, 1964.

Woods, Donald A. "Weeding the Library Should Be Continuous," *Library Journal* LXXVI (August 1951), pp. 1193-96.

5

RECOMMENDED WEEDING OBJECTIVES

INTRODUCTION

It seems evident that the objectives of weeding should help fulfill the basic objectives of the library. Libraries claim to have specific, clear-cut goals, but in practice they are likely to have vague, generalized objectives. These objectives, while rarely stated clearly or considered in day-to-day decision making, still seem to be in the minds of those administrators running libraries.

Depending upon the library, these objectives might include: supporting school, college, or university curriculum; supporting research efforts in university or special libraries; supplying recreational, informational, and educational services and materials in public libraries; supporting the aims of some larger institutions, as in the case of special libraries; or serving as centers or repositories of civilization's heritage, as with national and major regional libraries. In no case does weeding reduce the ability to fulfill these objectives. On the contrary, weeding seems to increase accessibility, improve efficiency, reduce costs, and in many other ways improve collections and services to the average user. Even though libraries have goals that vary considerably, they all might gain by using the same general weeding objectives, which could be varied quantitatively depending upon the needs of the clientele.

GOALS RELATING TO WEEDING

It is suggested that the following goals relating to weeding should be considered by libraries:

The primary collection areas are to consist of a core collection of books (and other materials) most likely to be used by the clients. ("Primary collection areas" refers to the open stacks, areas accessible to users, or the other library areas housing the readily available collections.)

The remainder of the books, least likely to be used (the non-core collection), are to be located in secondary storage areas, removed to other libraries, or discarded, depending upon the major objectives of the library and the potential value of the non-core collection. ("Secondary storage areas" refers to compact storage, depository storage, or areas that are less accessible than the primary areas and that represent less expensive storage space.)

The core collection is to retain _____% of the likely future use of the present collection. (The percentage is to be filled in individually for each library, depending upon its objectives and the possible unfavorable impact of lost usage upon the clients.) If conditions warrant, the core collection may be broken down into sub-collections by types of material, location, department, service, or in any other convenient way. For example:

1. Reference is to retain _____% of its anticipated future use.

2. The fiction collection _____%.

3. Adult non-fiction _____%.

4. Art is to retain _____%.

5. The Dewey 900's are to retain _____%.

6. Microfilm is to retain _____%.

7. Periodicals are to retain _____%.

8. Branch libraries are to retain'_____%.

PROBLEMS RELATING TO THESE OBJECTIVES

In order to implement the above objectives, two immediate problems must be solved.

First, how are the percentages of anticipated future use of a collection to be determined? That question will be answered rather precisely in future chapters. At this point it should be assumed that these percentages can be determined both accurately and practically.

The second problem cannot be dealt with so easily. What percentage of the future usage of a collection should one hope to retain with the core collection? This question entails both personal judgment and practical considerations. Conservative judgments are called for.

An arbitrary figure must be selected. A small public library does not risk much if it retains 95 percent of the anticipated future circulation of the present fiction collection; in fact, even 90 percent might be reasonable.

However, as the data develop, certain practical considerations may assist in making such decisions. In Table 1, from the *Five Libraries Study* made by this author in 1969, 96 percent of the anticipated future use of the Briarcliff fiction can be retained with 56 percent of the present fiction collection. Ninety-nine percent can be retained with 84 percent of the collection. If the library is pressed for space, and if the additional gain of shelf space is more important than the possible 3 percent loss in usage of this material, then perhaps 96 percent would be a reasonable retention figure. However, if weeding out 16 percent of the collection will solve the current space problem, perhaps it would be better judgment to retain 99 percent of the future use.

Table 1
SHELF-TIME PERIODS OF THE CIRCULATION AND COLLECTION SAMPLES COMPARED (%)

Cumulative Shelf-Time Period (Mos.)	Briarcliff Circulation	Briarcliff Collection	Tarrytown Circulation	Tarrytown Collection	Morristown Circulation	Morristown Collection	Trenton Circulation	Trenton Collection	Newark Circulation	Newark Collection
0	72	22	69	24	87	41	55	12	49	14
1	79	30	77	34	93	52	65	16	62	19
2	85	37	83	42	97	56	70	20	70	22
3	86	41	85	47	–	60	76	22	75	26
4	90	47	88	51	98	63	79	24	78	29
5	94	52	89	55	–	65	80	27	81	32
6	96	56	91	58	–	68	82	29	83	34
7	97	64	93	61	99	71	85	31	84	36
8	–	68	–	62	–	72	86	33	–	39
9	98	70	94	65	–	74	–	35	87	41
10	–	72	97	67	100	75	88	37	88	42
20	99	84	98	82	–	84	93	53	95	60
30	100	92	–	89	–	90	–	61	97	70
40	–	96	99	94	–	93	97	67	99	74
50	–	99	–	96	–	96	–	72	–	78
60	–	–	100	97	–	–	98	74	–	83
100	–	100	–	99	–	97	99	80	100	92
200	–	–	–	–	–	–	–	92	–	98
300	–	–	–	100	–	100	100	97	–	–
400	–	–	–	–	–	–	–	99	–	100
600	–	–	–	–	–	–	–	100	–	–

SUB-OBJECTIVES RELATING TO THE MECHANICS
OF MEASURING MEANINGFUL SHELF-TIME PERIODS

In order to assist the entire weeding process, a series of sub-objectives have been recommended. The additional objectives aim: to build in practical safeguards against discarding needed materials; to create meaningful data; and to develop reports about weeding experience that would be useful to others.

In this book, the basic criterion involved in making decisions for keeping or weeding is called "shelf-time period." This period estimates or measures the length of time a book remains on the shelf between successive uses. The author has found, as a result of his studies, that this criterion is the best predictor of use of a book. The following objectives should be used selectively by individual libraries, depending upon their individual needs, wants, resources, and long- or short-term goals.

That records or controls be established, so that shelf-time periods can be identified. This may be done by any method that would indicate and record circulation and in-library use of library materials.

Mechanically, it can be done by using and keeping intact the circulation records developed when using the book-card method of circulation control; by the use of coded circulation-indicating dots on the back of the book card when using the transaction system for circulation; or by circulation date print-outs for computer circulation systems.

There are several other methods that may be used. The current move toward the transaction card system of circulation control, often with no easily available indication of an individual book's circulation activity, needs to be modified or augmented so that such information becomes available.

Records for non-circulating materials (reference works, reserved collections, bound periodicals, etc.) must be kept if such materials are to be weeded using shelf-time period. This often requires new techniques, records, or procedures.

That procedures and techniques be established that would simplify the compilation of shelf-time period data for individual volumes or materials. For example, when book cards are filled up and there is no space to indicate a new date due, they are frequently removed and replaced with new cards. This destroys the use of data. Such old cards should be left in the book, or the last date of use should be transcribed from the old card onto the new card.

A second example would be the application of a coded mark on the spine showing use. Then use data could be observed without removing a book from the shelves.

That shelf-reading be done on a regular basis so that all volumes in the entire collection will be in correct classified order. To the user, a misshelved book is equivalent to a lost book. If no use occurs because a book is improperly shelved (and thus not accessible to the user), such a title is likely to be weeded under the shelf-time period criterion. Whether this weakens the collection appreciably needs to be examined more closely.

That use data be recorded and preserved as carefully as is reasonably possible. This means that circulation desk personnel must be careful and accurate when charging books in and out. This objective has been included for two reasons.

It is obvious that careless data will cause the weeding of volumes or materials that should not be weeded and the keeping of other materials that should have been weeded. Careless data control can destroy the validity of this whole procedure.

Secondly, in a field study of circulation control made by the author in 1973, a check of the quality of the work being done uncovered hundreds of errors. Unless people realize the importance of careful work and unless they are trained and supervised, the level of performance is likely to be poor.

That books from locked and inaccessible collections, which are to be weeded, be placed upon the open shelves or in primary storage areas before a decision is made on their removal from the collection. It was found, as might be expected, that such materials are not able to compete for user attention with the rest of the collection. If weeding is contemplated, the books should be tested in the marketplace of normal use.

An in-depth study of books located in restricted storage areas showed that usage was one-fourth that of similar titles located on open shelves.[1] Perhaps the restricted books should be returned to open stacks since such restrictions reduce their value. The purpose of relocating books is defensive: to prevent the discarding of books that would have been identified as being part of the core if they had been stored differently.

The reshelving period should not be less than a shelf-time that would be represented by a circulation shelf-time period to include 95 percent of the future use, or whatever other percentage might have been predetermined for the keeping level.

That libraries establish written objectives yearly which relate to the purposes of weeding. Weeding can be done for many reasons, and the exact reasons become important in the decision-making processes involved in the weeding procedures. When the library's greater goals are clearly defined, levels of weeding or non-weeding become easier to determine.

That libraries should annually establish the exact level of future use to be retained by the present collection. This can be determined for the library as a whole or for individual parts of the collection. (See p. 167.) The decision should be made in advance.

That the public card catalog be weeded annually so that it more nearly reflects the library's holdings. This also implies that shelf-lists and other listings be kept up to date. This is a necessary step if collections are to have adequate and accurate catalog accessibility and are to reflect more accurately the library's collection (See page 165 for a different point of view.)

Implicit in the need for weeding of catalogs is the necessity of periodic book inventories. (See page 166.)

That inventory be taken at least once a year and unintentional gaps in the collection be filled in. Since the suggested criterion for weeding is past use, the absence of books from the collection due to theft or loss will result in distorted shelf-time data for remaining works, and the core collection concept will be distorted. The distortion of data works in two ways.

First, a missing volume affects use of other works. If a user seeks information in a volume that is missing (the preferred work), he may look for the information in another book. That book, which ordinarily might not have had a recorded use, will now show a use at the expense of the preferred volume.

Second, it is impossible to know if a lost book should be identified as part of the core collection.

Therefore, it must be recognized that, since data can be collected only for books in the existing collection, it is necessary for the library to attempt to replace missing books meant to be in the collection.

If Volume 2 of the *World Book Encyclopedia* were lost, it would be recognized that the entire set was an integral part of the collection and the missing volume would be replaced. Subjective judgment is called for in determining which books to replace in the collection in the absence of shelf-time data, but it is the same judgment used in the initial ordering of new books, which is a normal part of the book selection process.

That libraries keep records on characteristics of the collection or the library that directly affect the use of materials, thereby altering the composition of the core collection. It is apparent that while use is the best predictor of core collections, many things affect usage.

Use is affected by accessibility, location in the library, height of the shelves, seasonal variations, appearance of the volumes, form of the materials, special shelving, librarians' recommendations, special promotion, bibliographies, dust covers, loan periods, reserved collections, etc. As an objective, it is suggested that each library keep records for one year on some variable and quantify its effect upon usage. Such variables that affect usage, were they known, could help to maximize circulation, to change the composition of the core collection (perhaps by making it smaller), and to produce a knowledge base replacing the intuitive base now used by librarians for many decisions. For example, if books at eye-level are used more than books on top and bottom shelves, the core collections, if kept in their present locations, will still satisfy the predicted future use; however, the core collection and the library will not have maximized the usage of the total collection. If such collections were on shelves which somehow could change their relative positions from time to time, a different and more satisfactory core collection would be likely.[2] One solution might be that no books should be stored on shelves where the location adversely affects book use.

A special set of problems besets university libraries. The impact of reserve collections, restricted collections, multiple library locations (departmental and undergraduate libraries, for instance), changes in curriculum, special assignments, long-term loan periods to faculty, all might affect the core collection concept. Yale University reports that their 4,000,000 volumes can be found in 64 different places,[3] and the University of Oxford, England, owns more volumes and has even more physical locations for them (72).

SUMMARY

The purpose of these objectives is to clarify exactly what a library wishes to do about weeding and to make weeding easier and more valid. The objectives for weeding listed above should be chosen to coincide with each library's goals. The sub-objectives begin to offer a method for meaningful weeding.

REFERENCES

1. Stanley James Slote, "The Predictive Value of Past-Use Patterns of Adult Fiction in Public Libraries for Identifying Core Collections" (unpublished Ph.D. dissertation, Rutgers University, 1970). University Microfilms, Inc., Ann Arbor, MI, No. 71-3104, p. 116.

2.   Stacks that revolve in such a way that shelf-positions keep changing are now found in some book stores. Their purpose is to prevent shelf location from adversely affecting sales.

3.   Lee Ash, *Yale's Selective Book Retirement Program* (Hamden, CT: Archon Books, 1963), p. xi.

6

APPROACHES TO WEEDING

A number of different general approaches to weeding have been given serious attention. These are:

Subjective weeding. This method involves a series of rules, principles, or guides that require for implementation subjective judgment on the part of the weeder. This is the most common form of weeding found in libraries today.

Age. With this method of weeding, books are removed from the shelves according to the date of imprint, copyright, or acquisition. Such age data are often used to assist decision-making when doing subjective weeding. Future usage patterns can be reliably predicted when age is used as a criterion (p. 65, #2).

Shelf-time period. The length of time a book remains unused on the shelf between circulations is called its shelf-time period. This method is often used intuitively together with subjective criteria.

Mathematical approaches. Several complex formulas or models have been suggested which, in fact, utilize information covered by the methods listed above. To date, these have been theoretical suggestions of questionable validity.

Combined criteria. The use of shelf-time period and imprint date, or any other combination of criteria, has been investigated and utilized in weeding. Such combinations have not been found to improve the quality of weeding.

PROBLEMS ENCOUNTERED USING THESE APPROACHES

Each of these approaches presents serious difficulties. The following is an attempt to outline the problems.

Subjective weeding. When weeding using subjective criteria, the weeder has selected criteria satisfactory to himself but unsubstantiated by objective evidence. If two experienced weeders are given the same collection to weed, widely differing collections of weedable volumes are likely to be identified.

In addition, the procedure is a lengthy one. Since weeding is considered to be a professional task, it is left, in small libraries especially, to a professional who already has many other responsibilities. It is not uncommon that the weeding procedure may take two or three years in a public library. It is also not uncommon, under these circumstances, that a weeding program has been started and left unfinished when enthusiasm has flagged. The methodology in subjective weeding is to make up rules that *seem* rational and apply them in a way that *seems* reasonable.

Age. When using age as a criterion for weeding, several decisions must be made before weeding can start. It must be decided what date is to be used. The following are some of the dates that can be employed:

1. Copyright date. The date used can be the earliest, the most recent, or an average of these two dates. It can be a date reflecting a major reworking of a title, a revised edition, or a new edition.

2. Imprint date. Here again the date used may be the first or last imprint date of a volume. Sometimes no copyright of a work exists and the only date available is the imprint date.

3. Purchase or acquisition date. If the "newness" of a volume is to be judged by some date, the purchase date or acquisition date could give more accurate information than copyright or imprint dates for the collection in question.

   An even more reasonable date would be the date the book was shelved. It has been suggested that when using the book card system of circulation control, the original shelving date be the first date entered on the card. Such dating would simplify subsequent data interpretation.

4. Date originally written or published. This date reflects the age of a work but not the age of a volume. If more newly created works are the ones that are used most, such a date might well be significant. However, newer editions of classics tend to be used more than older, especially as typeface and size improves.

5. Some other date. A date that a volume is rebound, for example, might be of significance.

Once the desired date is selected, two serious questions remain. What date is to be used if a title is to have all of its volumes considered together? Where does one find the date desired, and is it a practical source? The problem of multiple volumes for one title is not serious if these are different editions and are treated as separate works. Generally, a new edition of a classic will be preferred to an older edition. Therefore, it is advisable to consider volumes independently rather than as a group.

However, if all similar titles are to be considered together, the decision of which date to use becomes a major problem, since a weeding decision might be hard to apply. There does not appear to be a satisfactory solution to this difficulty.

The difficulty in determinng what date to use manifests itself in other ways. If titles are to be considered as a group, all of the copies of the same title held by the library must be uncovered. The card catalog or shelf-list will be the authority but will not indicate that a cataloged volume has been stolen or otherwise removed from its normal place. In addition to reading the shelves, all date-due records will have to be checked. If the volume itself lacks dates, a bibliographic search to determine when it was written, printed, or published will be required.

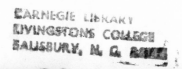

Shelf-time period. There are three major methods of developing shelf-time period (discussed in detail in part 2), and each of these has its problems both in the development of the criterion and in its application. What follows is a selective summary.

1. *Shelf-time periods developed from book cards.* The book card system of circulation control presents a number of problems. When book cards are lost or used up and discarded, information is lacking. When information is given only for circulating volumes, it is difficult and time-consuming to create comparable data for non-circulating books.

2. *Shelf-time periods developed by marking spines.* When using this method, confidence in the data is weakened by the difficulties of controlling the accuracy of the spine-marking. The physical markings can be removed, obscured, or overlooked. Careless or disinterested personnel at the circulation desk can fail to make the proper marks. The spine-marking system is valuable, however, in that books can be weeded without opening them up or inspecting them in any other way.

   The spine-marking system is applicable to the non-circulating collection in libraries where all volumes used within the library could be spine-marked and reshelved by library personnel.

3. *Computer methods.* It is possible that for libraries using a computer circulation control system, programs could be developed to give print-outs of all the shelf-time periods of all the volumes that have circulated. This data could be manipulated further to report the cut-off date. Needless to say, the program, the print-out, and the hardware are expensive. Such a method of weeding has been suggested in the literature but is hard to find in actual use.

Mathematical approaches. The mathematical approach involves quantifying certain variables and computing them in a specified formula or equation. The method is difficult to understand and to apply, and the data are difficult to uncover; complex mathematics is misused in this situation. Morse[1] and Lister[2] both recommend this approach, but since their orientation is toward ultimate storage and comparative use costs, their method has more validity when applied to cost control than when applied to weeding.

Further, in the use of mathematical models, the accepted assumptions are quantified to give percentages, costs, or other specific units upon which to make decisions. From a practical point of view, these mathematical results tend to be far from reality, since, in general, a whole series of assumptions (themselves unproved and often untested) are quantified. The combining of a series of *assumptions* to give precise mathematical results is considered to be an invalid approach.

For example, certain of these formulas assume that, on the average, obsolescence increases with age. While this may be true, *on the average*, assuming a steady rate of obsolescence and using it in a decision-making formula compounds the error. Individual volumes differ from average behavior. A formula produced in this manner will lend an unjustified confidence to decision-making.

REFERENCES

1. Philip M. Morse, *Library Effectiveness: A Systems Approach* (Cambridge, MA: M.I.T. Press, 1968).

2. Winston Charles Lister, "Least Cost Decision Rules for the Selection of Library Materials for Compact Storage" (unpublished Ph.D. dissertation, Purdue University, 1967).

7

CORE COLLECTIONS FOR SPECIFIC TYPES OF LIBRARIES

INTRODUCTION

The following are some ideas that might prove helpful in creating the core collection percentage figures for different kinds of libraries and different types of materials. What percentage of present use should one aim to keep? It must be emphasized that the higher the use-percentage kept, the smaller the amount of weeded material. Nevertheless, even at the level of keeping 100 percent of the future use of a collection, weeding will still be indicated.

It is not easy to establish "keeping" percentages. The basic difficulty is that all of these percentages are based in part upon subjective judgment and are subject to change based upon experience.

SMALL PUBLIC LIBRARIES

By "small public libraries" is meant libraries that do not feel that they are the permanent storage centers for the world's heritage. They frequently have limited reference collections and minimal reference services. Typical are hundreds of big city branch libraries and the libraries in many cities of under 20,000 population. Their services are basically threefold: they supply recreational and informational reading to their clients; they serve as a supplement to the public school educational program; and they supply a limited number of reference works. The quality of the reference service is low, and the present patterns are such that 85 to 90 percent of the requests are for ready reference or simple reference questions.[1] Thus, small public libraries are performing a wide range of partial or low-level services, which society accepts.

Therefore, the core collection can be subdivided into rather broad areas without exposing society to great inconvenience. Limited experience in several such libraries indicates that weeding with four separate collection divisions is adequate. These four consist of:

1. Fiction, including mysteries, short stories, science fiction, and westerns.

2. Non-fiction; all the Dewey classifications combined as one class. Biographies are also included here.

3. Reference materials, including periodicals, newspapers, pamphlets, photographs, and other miscellaneous materials.

4. Archives; anything in the permanent collection.

Each of these areas tends to have shelf-time periods differing significantly from the others, yet within each group a certain reasonable consistency exists.

One might start by trying to retain 95 percent of the present usage for fiction, 97 percent for non-fiction, and 99 percent for reference; archives would not be weeded at all, except as the objectives of this collection might change.

A small project was undertaken by the author to observe the effect of combining fiction and non-fiction into one collection for weeding purposes, even though the weeding was not actually performed. It was decided to keep 97 percent of the anticipated future circulation. The impact on the separate classes was not unexpected. In the library studied, over 99 percent of the fiction used and about 93 percent of the non-fiction used would have been retained.

Furthermore, non-fiction would have had to be weeded more extensively than fiction. This result was not as disturbing as might at first appear. Fiction is likely to have a much longer useful life and be more valid as it gets older. Non-fiction (textbooks, for example) tends to be full of errors a few years after publication. In an average small public library, there are hundreds of classics in fiction but only a handful of useful classics in non-fiction.

Another aspect of small library weeding is that such weeding is unlikely to do much harm. The sale, donation, relocation, or destruction of the weeded collection has few dangers. However, it is suggested that special regional libraries be given an opportunity to add these weeded volumes to their permanent collections. An occasional volume may fill a gap in such a larger collection. It is also suggested that regional libraries make their collections more widely available to the average reader.

MAJOR PUBLIC LIBRARY RESEARCH COLLECTIONS

Much of what has been said about smaller public libraries also relates to those massive and outstanding research libraries that have developed in major urban areas. These include such libraries as the John Crear in Chicago, Enoch Pratt in Baltimore, the Newark Public Library, and many other large libraries located in the bigger cities. They are frequently trying to perform two distinct functions.

One function is to serve as the popular public library, satisfying a number of recreational, educational, and ready reference functions. In these areas, weeding may follow the general pattern of the small public library. In the *Five Libraries Study*, it was found that an outstanding collection, such as that of Newark, had lower circulation figures in fiction than the smaller collection in the Morristown, New Jersey, Public Library, which contained one-quarter the number of fiction volumes. Insofar as it operates as a local circulator of popular materials, weeding can keep 95 to 99 percent of the anticipated future use without denying patrons what they want.

The second important function, that of a regional resource and reference center, calls for the use of higher keeping levels for the core collection or perhaps a different approach to weeding. For example, in a regional resource center it is likely that none of the books should be discarded unless they are either duplicates or are being replaced with the same or similar material. Furthermore, much of the material being weeded might well be retained in secondary storage areas. It is good practice to determine in advance the number of duplicates that are to be retained. Some libraries protect their collections by retaining two copies of a title.

Reference and information collections may have even greater limitations put upon them. Depending upon the level of the reference services it is called upon to perform, no weeding should be done except for replacing certain works with newer editions or more definitive works. Even here, out-of-date editions often become important resources.

However, with massive research and reference collections, it is frequently the case that one part of the collection is more accessible than other parts. Often a closed stack area exists. The weeding procedure may then identify reference works that are likely candidates to be removed from the open stacks and re-established in the closed stack area. Certainly for important, large, heavily used reference collections, the core collection should satisfy at least 99.5 to 100 percent of the anticipated use.

MEDIUM-SIZED PUBLIC LIBRARIES

Little information needs to be added for those libraries that fall between the above two groups. Many medium-sized centralized libraries are characterized by a dual role of the major library; often the branches are the popular circulation libraries and the downtown central branch is a resource and reference center. The degree to which these libraries are used should determine the characteristics of the core collections. As with major resource centers, the library might be more interested in replacing lost and stolen books than in weeding out current holdings. The usage, objectives, and client expectancy should help determine weeding levels.

Where public libraries of any size have divided subject responsibility for collections or have specialized collections of value, it is obvious that weeding must be considered in the light of the library's goals.

PUBLIC SCHOOL LIBRARIES

It is the often-stated objective of school libraries that they support the curriculum of the school. Other goals involve services to staff, administrators, and parents. In actuality, many of these libraries are used mostly as study halls, and the understaffing of these libraries has been notorious.

Basically, school libraries are acting as self-service supermarkets, and their direct services hardly touch the individual student. As Berelson pointed out, only 40 percent of the books children borrow come from the school library.[2]

Of all the types of libraries, school libraries lend themselves most to weeding. However, they are the most reluctant to remove out-of-date and unused materials. In the face of their overwhelming problem of undersupport, school libraries have failed to prevent the landslide of students from descending upon the public library. As courses and syllabuses change, as new subjects appear and old disappear, as students' interests and awareness broaden, great challenges are presented to school libraries.

The fact that school libraries are able to accept only a limited part of the responsibility means that they can be weeded in depth without seriously affecting the users. Collections and services are defective and will continue to be inadequate until school libraries have eight or ten times their present resources. They do not have any responsibility to preserve the national heritage, to be definitive research resource centers, or to be complete or comprehensive in any area.

As far as the recreational collections are concerned, it is suggested that school libraries try to retain 90 percent of anticipated future use and buy heavily to build up greater usage, since what is newest is what tends to have the greatest demand.

In the area of the reference collection, 95 percent is adequate, since supplemental collections are to be used anyway. Even the most perfunctory look at school libraries reinforces the opinion that deep weeding would improve collections.

One of the advantages a school library has in developing weeding criteria is that one year's use patterns are generally adequate for prediction unless new courses have been added to the curriculum. Conversely, lack of use in one year is often the first indication to the librarian that a course has been dropped. The one-year natural cycle means that the weeding criteria can almost always be developed within one year without worrying about long-range cyclical influences. This is a characteristic not found in other types of libraries, with the possible exception of undergraduate college libraries.

JUNIOR COLLEGE LIBRARIES

Everything said about the school library might be considered valid to some degree for the junior college library. In general, the main problem here is in building up, rather than reducing, the size of the collection. Since many of these libraries are new, less weeding may be called for. In addition, weeding seems to present less risk than in other libraries, for two reasons.

In the first place, a large number of courses generate relatively little use of library material. This may be a result of the more practical nature of the terminal courses. These libraries have only a very small influence on a large segment of their students.

Secondly, the yearly cycle helps to accelerate decision-making and adds confidence in identifying materials not likely to be used again. Thus, a reasonable standard for core collections would be one that would satisfy between 90 percent and 95 percent of the anticipated future use. To date, no important research project on weeding has treated school or junior college libraries.

COLLEGE AND UNIVERSITY LIBRARIES

The focus of most weeding research has been upon college and university libraries, since this is where many of the most serious problems exist. Many such libraries have had critical space shortages because they lack the financial resources necessary for expansion. Rapid growth of the major universities (and their libraries), financial pressures due to increased costs and decreased donations, increase in the number of advanced degrees awarded, and recent cutbacks of government support have forced these libraries to seek relief.

For years university libraries have projected the image of the collectors and preservers of knowledge. It is not true, however, that these libraries are solely repositories of the great national and human heritage. Collections of old textbooks, workbooks, out-of-date and useless non-fiction, low quality giftbooks, and books that have never been used at all abound in most of these collections. Therefore, it is suggested that in non-research collections, such as fiction, textbooks, etc., weeding be done as it is elsewhere, keeping in the core collection those works likely to retain 95 percent of their future usage.

In the remainder of the collection, weeding can be applied at any reasonable level, since transfer from primary to secondary storage should be the basic form of disposition of non-core works. Where no other factors are involved, the 97 percent future use level is recommended.

One other kind of weeding of main collections is possible. When departments have independent or geographically decentralized collections, it is possible to remove a complete section of the main library to such separated libraries in the system. Of course, such action must be based upon clear-cut objectives relating to the ease of access desired and the resources of money, space, and personnel available. Duplication of collections in the main branch and its departmental libraries is expensive, but it improves the access dramatically.

The overlapping nature of modern disciplines and the interdisciplinary character of many courses complicate the solution to easy access. Departmental libraries increase accessibility to some and reduce it to others, unless considerable duplication of materials exists.

Even in monolithic libraries, where no departmental libraries exist, materials are scattered rather widely. This occurs because of types of format (books, oversized books, pamphlets, microfilm, periodicals, AV materials); age of material (different runs for older materials); new book displays; archival collections; condition or state of processing (new books, periodicals being bound, books partially cataloged, temporarily lost volumes, etc.); special needs (reserve collections, circulating and non-circulating collections, government documents); and divisions within one library. One can logically locate similar subjects in dozens of different places in a large library — a fact that reduces easy access. When duplication is used to facilitate access, the space problem worsens.

Since "easy accessibility" does not seem to be a major objective in many of the massive libraries, secondary storage may have little serious effect on the overall level of service. Use of secondary storage might well increase accessibility to the primary collection to such a degree that overall service is improved.

While generally a 97 percent core collection keeping level is called for, weeding in much greater depth is not completely out of the question. The weeding level for these libraries may be determined by other practical considerations. It may be that the number of volumes currently held in primary storage completely fills up the library, so that no additional space is available. Instead of predetermining the keeping level on the basis of usage, one can determine the number of volumes to be retained in the primary storage area stacks, and accept whatever level of future use this will produce.

For example, if the Briarcliff Public Library needed to get along with 70 percent of the present shelving space, it would keep 98 percent of its present usage.[3] The secondary storage areas available could be used for determining such levels. There should not be more books transferred to secondary storage than can be stored conveniently. The size of the core collection may also be decided by determining the most economic mix of primary and secondary storage, considering all the costs involved for book removal, library maintenance, cost of services, etc.

As large libraries grow, these more practical considerations can be taken into account and careful research should be undertaken to help in the decision-making processes.

SPECIAL LIBRARIES

Librarianship in general has been hurt by attempting to group a large miscellaneous, dissimilar group of libraries into one class and calling them "special libraries." At best, there is a very tenuous similarity between the various types of special libraries. How do large legal libraries relate to small stock photography libraries? How do hospital, music, and newspaper libraries interrelate? Their materials, staff, size, objectives, and services frequently bear no visible relationships.

It is suggested that the various types of libraries might create their own concepts of core collections. Even within individual types, sub-types would be required. Clearly, then, each library must be considered in terms of its objectives—those relating both to its materials and services, and to the alternatives available.

For example, some newspaper libraries not only clip and file their own newspaper but also index it. Obviously, older clippings can be weeded with much less exposure when an index exists.

Criteria can be developed. National news, well indexed and reported elsewhere, can be weeded in depth without exposure. The general technique advocated here, that of anticipated use, can still be valuable and is perhaps the best approach to creating weeding criteria for special libraries.

In one weeded library, 100 percent of anticipated future use was accepted, and still 90 percent of the items were in the non-core collection.[4] Most special libraries lend themselves to weeding in depth, even though generalized keeping levels are hard to recommend for special libraries as a group.

As with archives, the objectives often prevent weeding of special materials on the basis of shelf-time period. One example was found by the author in a music publisher's library, where all copyrighted songs, sheet music, records, original manuscripts, etc., were retained. This was the stock in trade of the main business, and legal or financial matters could arise from any music holding, no matter how long its shelf-time period.

LIBRARY SYSTEMS

Ideally, public library systems have the advantage that certain centralized services can make weeding in depth less threatening to the integrity of the combined collections. Centralized or regional resource centers could be responsible for holding unique but little-used volumes.

Perhaps the best tool to encourage weeding is a union catalog. The easy accessibility of works at a neighbor's library reduces the need to hold many questionable volumes. When union catalogs are combined with telephone interlibrary loan and pick up and delivery service, members of systems often take on some of the characteristics of branches, and they can weed at the 90 to 95 percent use level.

SUMMARY

The purpose of this chapter is to give some guidelines for determining the acceptable level of use retained by core collections. It can be seen that librarians must use considerable judgment, experience, and professionalism in achieving this.

Under the proposed methods, these judgments are limited to judgments of objectives, goals, and services to be given rather than individual titles to be saved or weeded. At the worst, it gives us two groups of books: the core collection, from which *no* volumes will be weeded, and the non-core collection, from which *all* the weeded volumes will be selected.

Real judgment is also essential in disposing of the weeded volumes, in evaluating secondary storage, and in following up on the success of a weeding program. This total approach does not lower the professionalism of librarianship, but raises it. It replaces the present primitive technique of selecting titles or volumes for weeding with a quantified criterion, created through objective observation.

REFERENCES

1.   William A. Katz, *Introduction to Reference Work, Vol. II: Reference Services* (New York: McGraw-Hill, 1969), p. 38.

2.   Bernard Berelson, *The Library's Public* (New York: Columbia University Press, 1949), p. 11.

3.   Stanley James Slote, "The Predictive Value of Past-Use Patterns of Adult Fiction in Public Libraries for Identifying Core Collections" (unpublished Ph.D. dissertation, Rutgers University, 1970). University Microfilms, Inc., Ann Arbor, MI, No. 71-3104, p. 79.

4.   Stanley J. Slote, "An Approach to Weeding Criteria for Newspaper Libraries," *American Documentation* XIX (April 1968), p. 172.

8

ANALYSIS AND REVIEW OF THE LITERATURE OF WEEDING

PURPOSES FOR A STUDY OF THE LITERATURE

There has been a massive quantity of material published on the subject of library weeding. Almost 1,000 use studies can be identified, if one adds the more current works to Jain's list of 631 works.[1] From this mass there have been selected reports that add substance to the specific approaches used in this book. These selected reports represent the background for the present work, which has attempted to take another step forward.

The purpose or motivation behind the production of a book or article often becomes rather clear upon reading it. Its purpose affects its tone and content. There are many reasons for studying or adding to the literature of a subject:

To compare what one is doing with what is being done elsewhere in the field.

To look for hard facts—real evidence that would cause one to reinforce or discard certain accepted techniques.

To uncover limitations of the knowledge in a field in order to undertake research, starting from the present knowledge base.

To examine the suggestions of thinkers in the field, in order to give direction to further thought and study.

To read of the experience of others as a guide to identifying pitfalls to be avoided.

To find out specifically how to perform certain operations.

To keep current with the literature.

To create new knowledge in the field.

CRITICISM OF LIBRARY LITERATURE

Two characteristics of the literature in librarianship (and weeding in particular) are that there is little cumulation of knowledge, and that there is no consistency in the objectives of the overall literature in the field. Current articles frequently show no knowledge of the history and past thought in the subject. It is a serious criticism of the literature of librarianship, including the more than 700 periodicals in the field, that articles currently appearing could have been written 15 to 75 years ago. Editors accept such articles without limitation or discrimination.

What is needed is not only the publication of the first stirrings of new knowledge, hard facts, tendencies and information gained from experiment, and careful observation, but also a willingness on the part of readers to accept what is known.[2] It has been known for at least 19 years that shelf-time period is the best criterion for identifying core collections. Yet, many articles and books published in the years since do not accept this finding, which apparently has been one of the best-kept secrets in librarianship.

The first criticism of the literature of librarianship concerning weeding, core collections, and shelf-time period is that the literature has had little impact on the practitioners, teachers, and leaders in the field. It is possible that the very mass of publications has blocked the view of what is significant.

What is *needed* are facts, data, or ideas that will stimulate the serious student or the practitioner to better his performance and enlarge his knowledge in the field. The following section makes an attempt to classify some of the literature. What has been said about the literature of weeding might well be repeated for almost any topic in librarianship.

CHARACTERISTICS OF THE LITERATURE

In much of the literature of weeding and library usage, there is a similarity in the type of works published year after year. In general, these types of works can be characterized as follows:

Repetitive. Repetition can be one of three kinds—either the actual reprint of an article that has been published before; summaries or analysis of previous works; or a fresh presentation of what has been said before, with little credit given to the originator. While a certain amount of repetition might be helpful for the learning process, librarians have been bombarded with repetitions of the same old, and perhaps invalid, ideas for 100 years.

"How-to" literature. "How-to" articles are generally authoritative but give little evidence, few facts, and no sources. A better way to do something is claimed, even though it is frequently a method that has been alternately recommended or rejected throughout the decades! The ultimate authority is personal judgment, often not even supported by a simple literature search or by the most basic attempts to compare two different techniques. One interesting characteristic of this kind of work is the conflict and disagreement that it creates among the authorities.

Scholarly historical summary. Such work is generally a carefully documented study of the past literature of the subject, usually selective, in order to emphasize the development of the field and the best practices. This kind of article has form, meaning, and usually a good point. It is a short-cut for a new student in the field, and might be considered a guide to the best literature of a subject.

Broad philosophy. This is an attempt to synthesize past knowledge and to reinforce newer valid concepts. It always has some strong base for the concepts contained, often the most recent research reports or new technologies (computers and advanced math, for example). This approach tends to make its points in an organized way, as contrasted to the authoritative approaches.

Controlled study. A controlled study is a carefully planned, scholarly attempt to uncover new knowledge. It is a sicentific, experimental approach with enough of the data, background, methodology, and techniques reported so that the experiment can be replicated. It uses the "scientific method," with an attempt to observe one variable at a time. The conclusions follow directly from the data, and the range of their reliability is clearly defined. Where variables are not being manipulated by the researcher, an attempt is made to be unobtrusive and avoid having the observation affect the results. Usually the claims made for the findings are modest.

PROBLEMS IN THE APPLICATION
OF THE LITERATURE

The literature of weeding is characterized by a number of other general problems:

1. There is a great variety in the quality, style, and value of the articles. This mix, even within the confines of one publication, must make one wary about the quality of the editing of even the best of the scholarly journals.

2. In general, there has been a lack of cumulative study in the field. Strangely, there is a certain amount of repetition and replication of each of the new techniques that have been reported, as if no one ever starts where the last researcher left off. Nor have the researchers themselves seemed to develop knowledge banks of increased information.

3. Access to the literature through bibliographies and indexes is difficult, inefficient, and incomplete.

4. Very few reports are complete. Fragmentation is common. Articles omitting data, techniques, background, or meanings are the norm. The reader is unable to tell whether what has been omitted was invalid, was left undone, or was omitted by carelessness.

5. There is much opinion and little hard knowledge in the literature. A wide range of periodicals avoid articles with data, research, statistics, and methodology as being "too academic."

SUMMARY OF THE LITERATURE OF WEEDING

Criteria used. In general, the studies that follow have used two principal weeding criteria: 1) the age of a volume, and 2) the length of time a volume remains in the library between successive uses or the number of uses in a given period of time (shelf-time period).

Various dates have been used to represent the age of a volume: the publication date, the year of accession, and the copyright date. In addition, the language of the publication and its country of origin have been used as variables.

The above variables have also been used in combinations. However, shelf-time period has the most serious support, with respect to both the number of supporters and the validity of the research evidence.

Methods of recreating use patterns. There has been some discussion in the literature as to how to uncover the past patterns of book use in a library. Most of the studies relied upon the book cards for their information; several reconstructed the information needed during the study, with no reference to past records; often, a combination of these methods was used. Two major approaches have been suggested for reconstructing circulation patterns as described by shelf-time periods.

1. The "historical reconstruction" approach is an attempt to record, in terms of the chosen variable, the entire use pattern of a volume since its acquisition in a library. When this method has been used, however, most researchers have limited their study to the last several years of use.

    The weakness of this method is that much of the important data may be missing. Cards from well-used books are often filled up and discarded, books are lost or stolen along with their book cards, charging systems are changed, and cards replaced. In general, the information available might be very unreliable.

2. The "current circulation" method looks at a very recent period of circulation (usually the most recent few days or weeks) and assumes that the present pattern of use at circulation is a valid sample of the total use pattern. Several such samples of circulation may be taken over a period of time and compared for consistency.

    The weaknesses here are that seasonal patterns might not show up, and that there are other factors that might make a short-term sample unrepresentative of the whole pattern. School assignments can change; different days of the week may have different use patterns; and the relative use (the percentage of the whole class represented by the sample) is disregarded. However, as techniques are developed to overcome these weaknesses, the "current circulation" method has become more and more the preferred method of recent researchers.

Aims of the studies. The scope of the studies was often restricted by the aim of the work, especially in the area of validating findings relating to weeding. Attempts were often made to find weeding criteria useful in identifying core collections.

However, studies were also made in order to justify automated circulation methods, to compute and compare the cost of various kinds of primary and secondary storage, to evaluate collections, to test mathematical formulas, and to limit the growth of active collections stored in the primary collection area. Therefore, the studies vary tremendously in their emphasis or lack of emphasis on weeding and its usefulness.

Findings of the studies. There has been a wide range of findings, and certain conflicting results have been reported.

1. In general, shelf-time period was found to be the most acceptable variable for identifying core collections. The methodologies and

assumptions were often validated with strong evidence for the superiority of the shelf-time period variable in predicting future use. Most studies agreed that this is the most valuable variable revealed.

2. The age of the volume was found to be somewhat predictive of future use, but generally of little practical value. Basically, the rejection of a small number of older volumes — the classics, which circulate with patterns similar to those of newer books — causes the age of volumes to be an inferior predictor of the future use.

3. Several explanations were found as to why shelf-time period produced a smaller core collection than the age of a volume.

4. Techniques for uncovering the information needed to produce weeding criteria have been simplified and improved.

5. Objective weeding was frequently recommended as a replacement for the subjective weeding most commonly used. Wherever controlled testing has been undertaken, the objective criteria have proven to be as valid as or more valid than subjective weeding.

6. No examples could be found where weeding was based solely on objective criteria; in every case some subjective criteria were added, often as an afterthought. Apparently it was emotionally difficult to weed using only objective criteria.

7. The problems of the growth of collections and the need for weeding were highlighted in almost every study. Weeding always appeared to be the solution, yet few reported that it had solved long-term shelf-space needs. Nor have any libraries reported a consistent *long-term* weeding effort.

THE LITERATURE REVIEWED

These reports have been divided into two groups — those based on judgment, which, in retrospect, proved to be valid judgment; and those based on research. The first group of studies has identified the problems that encourage weeding and has recommended approaches that have been later validated.

Studies identifying the problems.

1. **Eliot, Charles W.** The need for a criterion for thinning has long been a subject for discussion. Charles William Eliot, president of Harvard, outlined in 1902 the problems faced by university libraries.[3] After mentioning the rapid growth of libraries, he says:

> Under these conditions the great need of means of discriminating between books which may fairly be said to be in use and books which may fairly be said to be not in use has been forced on me, ...[4]

> I admit at once that the means of just discrimination between books in use and books not in use are not easy to discern or to apply; ...[5]

The concept in the first statement has been repeated many times in the literature. Eliot has hinted at the idea of using objective weeding criteria.

> Thus, it might naturally be suspected that a book which had not been called for in a university library for twenty years possessed but a faint vitality; ...[6]

2. **Ranck, Samuel.** In 1911, Samuel Ranck reported on a study he had made at the Grand Rapids Public Library,[7] one of the few use studies made in a public library. He stated the problem from the library administrator's point of view:

> Every circulating library of considerable magnitude that has been in operation for a number of years gradually accumulates many volumes that are seldom or never used.[8]

Ranck then presented data showing the "time since last use" for all the 64,162 volumes in the library. Among his findings were that 20 percent of the books had not circulated at all during the previous two years and 10 percent had not circulated in the previous five years. What is of particular interest is the similarity of his findings of more than 70 years ago compared with more recent findings (see Table 2). His 15.1 percent of fiction non-circulators compares closely to the figures of 12.1, 15.0, and 12.6 percent found for Briarcliff, Tarrytown, and Morristown collections of the *Five Libraries Study* (see p. 79).

Ranck pointed out the need for use studies:

> This problem of the unused book is one that will increase as the library grows older, and I believe that we cannot undertake the solution of it too soon or too carefully.[9]

3. **Ash, Lee.** Ash's report[10] is a summary of extensive and detailed studies made at Yale during a three-year period. It is an example of a middle-of-the-road study that followed both the folklore and the science of weeding. The study, which was used to establish practical guidelines for "the selective retirement program," combined objective weeding criteria with judgment and library expertise. Some of the conclusions parallel those of later and more detailed studies.

> If a book has been charged out on an average of once a year or more for the past five years, it should be considered "heavily used" material and should not be transferred....[11]

This criterion of *repetitive* use to identify core collections is not commonplace in the literature of weeding. Most of the studies have shown that a use once in five years (rather than once a year for five years) is a valid signal not to weed.

While not as detailed as one might wish, the report is really one of the most important available on the subject of weeding. It stresses one of the most troublesome problems faced by weeders—i.e., the problem that occurs when faculty and staff encounter such negative words and phrases as "selective book retirement program," "seldom-used scholarly books," "storage," "discarding," and "obsolescence."[12] Overcoming the emotional response to what should be an objective procedure remains an unsolved problem.

Table 2
COMPARISON OF DATA
RANCK 1911 VS. SLOTE 1969 COLLECTION CHARACTERISTICS

	Ranck	Briarcliff	Tarrytown	Morristown	Trenton	Newark
% of *fiction* not circulating in last two years	15.1	12.1	15.0	12.6	44.2	37.1

% Previously Charged Out

Shelf-Time Period	Total Collection		Fiction Only			
24 months	79.2*	87.9	85.0	87.4	55.8	62.9
60 months	90.4	99.7	96.8	96.5	73.5	82.7
120 months	95.8	100.0	98.9	97.7	82.8	92.9
204 months	98.6	-	99.8	100.0	92.2	98.0
300 months	99.0	-	100.0	-	97.2	99.8
312 months and over	100.0	-	-	-	100.0	100.0

*Figure for fiction was 84.9%.

In another direction, Ash approached the problem of the impact of storage on the overall use of the collection. He reported that in two years only 3⅓ percent of the library usage came from the stored collection. Therefore:

> ... the use of storage books at Yale is so limited that problems are not likely to occur in library service.[13]

A reasonably large part of this study dealt with various aspects of compact storage and the advantages of the Yale system. Ash included detailed cost data, and one of the major factors influencing the costs:

> Four and one half times as many books can be shelved by the Yale Compact Storage Plan as in conventional stack arrangement.[14]

He also reported a cost of storage at $0.61 per volume. This section of the work is invaluable for anyone considering compact storage, especially if it is studied along with Ellsworth's fine book.[15]

For the more conventional weeders, Ash offered strong support:

> In the actual process of selection for a book retirement program, we have found very little that can be reduced to a formula or routine.

> ... the execution of selective book retirement becomes increasingly a matter of knowledge, judgment and wisdom.

> [Weeding] cannot be determined solely on the basis of use.[16]

4. **Mueller, Elizabeth.** One of Mueller's substantial contributions was the identification of the characteristic that makes the age of a volume a poor predictor of future use.[17] Although more new titles were reported in circulation than older ones, on the average, in several cases she reported that certain older titles had circulation characteristics very similar to those of the new titles. This study, made in six public libraries, was an attempt to compare the non-fiction circulation characteristics of new versus old titles.

Mueller also reported on fiction circulation rates. Her rates of 4.4 to 7.3 circulations per volume per year can be compared to 2.8 to 6.2 volumes in this author's *Five Libraries Study*. Neither the size of the population nor the size of the collection correlates with this circulation characteristic.

5. **Buckland, M. K.** In a broader study at the University of Lancaster in England, it was suggested that libraries attempt to uncover " ... objective information about the best ways of providing a library service in a university."[18]

> [Traditional techniques] do not tell one how many books to buy, *how long to keep them* [italics mine], or how long the loan period should be.[19]

This study was an attempt to create computer-compatible mathematical models. Bradford's Law of Scattering[20] encouraged such an approach. One objective of Buckland's study was to determine "for how long should the documents, so painstakingly added to stock, be retained?"[21] It:

> ... showed that, in a petroleum library which can accommodate about 2,000 volumes, about 190 titles all retained for about 11 years would constitute the most useful stock pattern and would satisfy about 75% of the requests.[22]

Using a mathematical formula for evidence, Buckland concluded:

> ... effective is the policy of retaining heavily-used titles for a longer period than less heavily-used ones. In fact, as the usage of each volume declines with time there comes a point at which it would be cheaper to satisfy by interlibrary loan such requests as still occur rather than continue to incur storage costs.[23]

One of the assumptions of his formula—that the cost of discarding material is "trivial"—is a subject that needs considerably more study, as it has rarely been tested in a careful manner.

> ... in practice this might not be true, and the situation could arise where it is cheaper *not* to discard even if a document is totally unused.[24]

Then, turning to the subject of core collections, Buckland reported what is a rather well-known characteristic of libraries—that " ... 20% of the Lancaster stock generates 80% of borrowing."[25]

In this report, Buckland recognized the weakness of subjective weeding:

> It has been established that records of past use are the simplest and best available predictors of future use (considerably better than the unaided subjective judgment of either teachers or librarians); ...[26]

6. **Morse, Philip.** In his book,[27] Morse evaluated and reported on some of the findings of various studies made at M.I.T. He offered a series of concepts that he considered valuable for a discussion of the whole field of discarding books. He begins with a deceptively simple statement:

> ... the librarian should know, as accurately as possible, what now is going on and should be able to predict what probably will be going on in the future.[28]

This is the whole thesis of Morse's approach to weeding—the predictability of future usage. Morse wanted to discover the "pattern" of book use; he said that data necessary for such information could be obtained. Since it is expensive to obtain, however, it has not been done. In business, where such data becomes essential for decision-making, it is acquired. He noted that computer use would make it easier to gather such data.[29]

As with most of the practical research on weeding, Morse noted that one of the great unsolved problems of weeding has been:

> ... the traumatic one of destroying or otherwise getting rid of some of the less useful books, or the less drastic one of retiring some books to stacks or to deposit libraries, ...[30]

Nevertheless, he recognized the need for a solution and suggested that:

> ... it is important to be able to predict the future circulation of a book.... If one could retire only those books that had a chance of less than 1 in 6 or 1 in 10 of being asked for in the next year, the fraction of disadvantaged borrowers might be small enough to be endurable.[31]

Like most serious students of the subject, Morse reported that merely noting the age of a book does not take into consideration important use patterns displayed at M.I.T. He made the following statement:

> Thus, the conclusion that our year-by-year analysis led us, that the circulation behavior of a book depends (on an average) on its previous-year's circulation and not explicitly on its age or still earlier circulation, ...[32]

Morse pointed out that it would be advantageous to discover what data is needed for decision-making in weeding. He also reported on a study of book retirement based upon the criteria of age and non-circulation. By non-circulation, he refers to volumes with relatively long shelf-time periods. Using age as a criterion caused 5,200 inconveniences, while using non-circulation as a criterion caused only 3,600 inconveniences.[33]

> ... the [non-circulators] will circulate less often than the rest of the old books.[34]

7. **Slote, Stanley J.** This author[35] has conducted a use study involving non-book material. In most newspapers, metal "cuts" are used to produce the photographs that appear in print. These cuts are filed for reuse in case a person or event becomes newsworthy again. A systematic sample was taken from the entire collection. The conclusion was that no cut should be reused after the eighth year from its first use, provided that it had not been reused before. This meant that a shelf-time period of eight years would describe a core collection including all the cuts likely to be used in the future, provided that these cuts had been previously used only once.

It was also found that no cut had been used after its fourteenth year in the file, even if reused in the interim period. Ninety-two percent of the cuts had never been reused, an indication that better keeping criteria and procedures might have been called for. Thus, the age of the cut and/or the time between uses (shelf-time period) were combined to create the weeding criteria. Employing these criteria, 85 percent of the collection was weeded out.

This basic study alerted the author to the value of determining the "time between uses" (later called "shelf-time period"), which became the backbone of further research. This study was an example of the practical use of objective data for weeding.[36]

8. **Grieder, Elmer.** Grieder was one of the first to point out the value of being able to *predict* the impact of secondary storage on service to the client.[37] He sought to find out how many volumes might be stored without "serious detriment to service." He made some statistical counts similar to those suggested in this volume, first recording the "date of last circulation" of books at the circulation desk. He tabulated this data from the charge slips representing volumes in circulation,[38] then sampled the books on the shelves for the same variable. This information was then tabulated, as shown in Table 3.

Grieder's conclusion was that 39.2 percent of the books had not circulated in the previous 15 years and thus 76,656 volumes could have been stored in secondary areas "with no serious disruption of service." He stated that he could predict the amount of future use of volumes to be stored.

To validate this belief, Grieder made a two-week study of the books circulating, to determine the date of last circulation. He reported that if these

Table 3
GRIEDER STUDY*, 1949

STANFORD UNIVERSITY LIBRARY
SHELF-TIME PERIODS OF THE CIRCULATION AND COLLECTION
SAMPLES COMPARED (%)

Date of Last Circulation	Cumulative Shelf-Time Period	
	Collection	Circulation
1949	22%	63%
1948	32	79
1947	39	85
1946	44	87
1945	47	88
1940-1944	61	93
1935-1939	71	96
1930-1934	78	98
1925-1929	83	99
1920-1924	88	
1915-1919	92	
1910-1914	95	
1905-1909	98	
1900-1904	99	
Before 1899	100	100

*Figures revised and simplified.

15-year non-circulators had been stored, only 4.01 percent of the circulating volumes would have had to come from storage. If the 56,375 volumes that had not circulated in 20 years had been stored, only 2 percent would have had to come from storage. This study is important in that it anticipated the conclusions made by later studies and uncovered the best techniques for the prediction of future demand.

9. **Cooper, Marianne.** This study reported on the practical application of objective and subjective weeding criteria.[39] After a rather thorough report on many of the previous studies in the area of weeding, Cooper reported on the application of Trueswell's approach (see page 77) to the collection at the Chemistry Library at Columbia in 1965.

The purpose of the study was to find a way to reduce the number of volumes on the accessible shelves in the library. The methodology was to observe 135 charge-out cards, and to tabulate the use patterns. The data presented was as follows:

99 percent had been borrowed at least once in the past 8 years.
97 percent had been borrowed at least once in the past 5 years.
95 percent had been borrowed at least once in the past 3 years.
71 percent had been borrowed at least once in the past 1 year.[40]

It was decided to keep in the active collection those borrowed at least once in the last five years and to transfer or store the rest. The faculty rechecked weeded volumes and returned to the active collection a number of the volumes selected. Thus, shelf-time period was not the sole criterion used for weeding; such criteria as reference value were also considered. This refusal to accept completely the objective criterion for weeding is not unusual.

10. **Houser, Lloyd J.** Much has been written about the age of volumes and the use of this element for identifying core collections. In 1944, Gosnell[41] produced the first serious study of this type for a university library.

A pilot study by Houser,[42] while not dealing with weeding, suggested that the reference collections of two public libraries might be evaluated by using the latest copyright date as well as by comparing their volumes with standard check lists. The Plainfield, New Jersey, Public Library and the Woodbridge, New Jersey, Public Library were the sample libraries.

Houser demonstrated the wide variation between the holdings in these two libraries and implied that the library with the more recent date-distribution might better serve its users. He mentioned four objections to the use of the date-distribution:

a. The nature of publishing is such that a new copyright date does not necessarily mean that the information in the latest edition of a book title is quantitatively or qualitatively better than an earlier edition of the same title ... [in fact there may be] ... no change in the content of the original book.

b. A number of titles remain standard works or are classics....

c. Some ... works with earlier copyright dates may very well serve as adequately as similar works with later copyright dates.

d. ... an older edition of a work ... may preclude the necessity of replacing it with its newer edition.[43]

Thus, this study highlighted some of the problems involved in using the imprint date as a weeding criterion.

Research Studies.

The remaining reprots are all serious research efforts that relate directly to weeding criteria and that deal with the variables of age of the volume, shelf-time period, or both. Purposes, methodology, data, and findings are reported in detail. In most cases, they are doctoral dissertations, funded research projects, or shorter reports on such projects. They are considered to be most significant.

1. **Lister, Winston C.** Lister's dissertation[44] is an interesting example of library research with a goal of practical application. It focused on uncovering the real costs involved in compact storage in order to determine whether such storage should or should not be used. Accepting the findings that the two best predictors of future usage are the age of the materials and the book usage rate, it studied the

economic impact that results when these two criteria are used to select books for compact storage.

The study, which deals with academic libraries, expresses the opinion that removal of materials from the working collection is a solution to the ever-growing university library. Such storing is of value to the patrons, since they are then " ... able to locate the bulk of their desired materials more easily and more quickly."[45] The study also attempted to uncover " ... some way of determining the optimal number of books which should be separated into storage."[46]

The Lister study, at three Purdue University branch libraries, consisted of taking a 20 percent sample of the titles from the shelf-list and tabulating use and age data by computer. A series of judgments were made concerning the costs of the various aspects of use and storage. These included building and equipment costs, maintenance and operating costs, circulation costs, and relocation costs. Formulas were developed to measure the total cost of using both criteria for decision-making. Since cost was the principal focus, weeding criteria were relegated to a rather junior position in this study.

The following conclusions are important:

> ... the author sincerely believes that selection of an item for storage should be based entirely upon its current (or immediate past) rate of usage.... As has been repeatedly pointed out in the literature, other measures of usage are not nearly so reliable as past history. In this research the age criterion, which is apparently the next best predictor of usage, was found to be far inferior to the usage rate criterion for scientific monographs.[47]

> ... there is evidence which illustrates extreme variability in the current usage rates of books of a common age, demonstrating the infeasibility of a single age-related obsolescence function....[48]

In addition, Lister affirmed two other points:

> It is possible to establish simple decision rules regarding the selection of library material for storage....[49]

Intellectual weeding policies, which require judgment and are based upon somewhat intangible variables, usually turn out to be time consuming, expensive, and qualitative attempts to predict future usage.[50]

Of particular interest is Lister's explanation of why the age criterion is faulty.

> The age model is based upon the average behavior of obsolescence with age.... The variability about the average rate of usage for each age group is completely ignored. It is because this dispersion about the mean is often very significant that causes some authors to protest a storage decision rule predicated upon the ages of books and to support the usage rate criterion.[51]

Concluding that some mechanical techniques could be very helpful, Lister maintained that computerized circulation systems would make the whole weeding process much easier, from the point of view of both selecting the volumes to be removed and altering the catalogs to reflect such moves.[52] As an alternative, he suggested that:

> It might become advantageous to mark, in some way, the outside covers of the books to provide usage rate indicators.[53]

2. **Silver, Edward A.** Silver's study[54] was part of a series of reports emanating from an operations research course at Massachusetts Institute of Technology. He pointed out the space problem facing the library:

> ... extra shelf space is rapidly diminishing due to the acquisition of new books. A possible course of action to remedy the situation is the use of weeding, ...[55]

Silver's approach was to investigate the effects of various decision criteria. His objective was to find a cut-point (a specific last date on a book card) that would enable the librarian to keep the number of books on the shelves at the same level, whenever it is applied. For example, if he wanted to keep 5,000 volumes on the shelves, he would find the cut-point that would give him this result.

Approximately 100 samples were chosen from eight different subject areas in the science library at M.I.T. These areas were: general science, math, physics, chemistry, geology, biology, engineering, and miscellaneous. The method decided upon was a systematic sample. The related variable was the "shelf-time since last circulation."

Among the conclusions were:

a. That the exclusive weeding policy should be based upon shelf-time since last use.

b. " ... that a criterion of this nature eliminates the need of technical aid in the weeding operation."[56]

c. That there are substantial variations among the different subject groups, in relationship to the selected variable.

d. That there is also a substantial variation from the mean within each group.

e. That books that never circulate or that contain no circulation data are a serious problem to the researcher in use studies of this kind.

Silver concluded that a weeding policy ought to be based upon the need for shelf space.

3. **Jain, Aridaman K.** Jain has produced two works that relate to book usage: the first is based upon pilot studies[57] and the second, a much more complete study, follows the leads uncovered in the pilot.[58]

In his pilot study, an interesting question was asked: what data can a librarian use to reconstruct usage patterns when historical records are not available? Jain was trying to identify criteria useful in selecting books for storage.

His methodology was to take a systematic sample of parts of the collection, using the shelf-list for selecting the sample. All the titles in current use during a five-week period, both at home and in the library, were recorded. An attempt was made to use the following as variables: a) language; b) country of publication; c) year of publication, and d) the year of accession. The method of evaluating the data was called "relative usage." It relates the number of titles being used in any category to the total number of volumes in the collection in the same category.

Although tables representing the data, the categories, and the findings (relative usage) were presented, no firm conclusions were reported, except that the findings could be used to make decisions for storing books. This exploratory study was an attempt to test a proposed methodology and a special approach.

In his more complete study, Jain pushed rigorously into the areas that he first explored in his pilot. His purpose was to study criteria that might be useful in determinng titles to be stored in secondary locations. With an emphasis on mathematical models, he examined all the previous work done and hoped to develop a better mathematical approach.

In this study Jain emphasized the importance of use studies. In support of this opinion he listed 631 works relating to book usage, discussing the more thorough and outstanding works.[59] His approach consisted of reviewing the previous work done, stating the weaknesses of these studies, and, through mathematical computation, developing a study without the same weaknesses. He covered 61 pages with mathematical proofs.

Jain's findings were two-fold. First, he was rather critical of all the previous studies, and stated their shortcomings in detail. Second, he offered his own formula. This is the "relative usage" found in the first study. Based upon this new approach, he concluded:

> In spite of the recent tendencies to overemphasize usage histories, this study shows that age is a significant variable in studying usage of monographs. As pointed out in this study, there are several problems associated with the usage histories of monographs and it is hard to say how much reliance can be placed on the usage histories under the current methods of record keeping. Also, while usage rates of individual monographs have considerable variation even over a short period of time, the usage rates of various age groups do not show any significant differences over time.[60]

The phrase "overemphasize usage history" was found in Jain's conclusions with no evidence found in his report that usage history was, in fact, studied by him and found wanting. This is the only study of significance that preferred to use age rather than usage as the criterion for weeding decisions.

4. **Fussler, Herman H., and Simon, Julian L.** Perhaps the most thorough research done in the area of use patterns has been by Fussler and Simon.[61] They noted that accumulative growth of collections causes serious space problems for many libraries. One approach to the problem is compact storage of books, storage which will not impede effective access to needed materials. A fundamental question they attempted to answer is:

> Will any kind of statistical procedure predict with reasonable accuracy the frequencies with which groups of books with defined characteristics are likely to be used in a research library?[62]

In order to select books for compact storage, this study endeavored to find a characteristic or variable that would predict which books were most likely and which least likely to be used.

The basic technique of the Fussler and Simon study was a modification (cross-sectional approach) of the historical approach to the past use of individual books.[63] The data came from the entire collection, as compared to the "current circulation method," in which the data came from the circulation desk only. The historical method ideally consists of recording the complete history of the past uses of the volumes, and ranking all of the volumes in accordance with the number of such uses per year. Since not all data were available, the authors modified this and used the "cross-sectional approach," recording all uses during previously determined periods of time, 5 years and 20 years. They assumed that future usage would continue at the same rate as in the past (though slightly reduced). They then related this use-ranking to the variables to be considered, such as age of the volume or date of last use. How "good" the function was, was judged in relationship to a book storage program. The "best function" is the one that identifies the fewest books in a core collection, which would maintain a predetermined level of use. In other words, the "best function" permits the storing of the most books at a given use level.

Several variables or functions have been studied. These include the following, either alone or combined:

a. publication date
b. accession date
c. language
d. use in last five years
e. years since last use

The study was further divided into three sections:

a. Functions for libraries with no records of prior use.
b. Functions that require five-year past due records.
c. Functions employing long records of past use.

A number of the conclusions in Fussler's study did not relate either to shelf-time period or to the age of a volume. The major findings that relate to these two variables are as follows:

It becomes evident that books can be separated into groups that will generate significantly different amounts of use. Because of the differences between the patterns of holdings in various matters and in various libraries, the effects of any given rule cannot be predicted without knowing more about the subject area and the library. But an inexpensive and quick set of surveys should in most cases provide all the information necessary for applying the rules successfully.[64]

... employing *years since last use* as the only variable, gives strikingly good results.[65]

... characteristics such as the age of a book and its language are less satisfactory in predicting future use than in past use. It is doubtful that any other variable will suddenly appear on the research scene and greatly increase predictive accuracy.[66]

Past use, where sufficient data are available, was found to be the best single predictor of the future use of a book.[67]

The variable of past use is sufficiently powerful that for libraries with 20-year use records the objective characteristics make little further contribution.[68]

Using the historical method, Fussler and Simon did get better results when a longer use history was projected. They implied that differences in libraries necessitate individual study for each collection,[69] and they attempted to combine variables to see if a better criterion would result:

Even if we consider the best of the rules that do not employ past use ... the results are not very satisfactory.[70]

Fussler and Simon also approached the question of whether there are better ways to select books for storage. They compared their criteria with the results obtained from the consensus of a group of scholars in a subject field. Without rejecting the validity of scholars' judgment, they concluded:

The various parts of the investigation convince us that with our rules we may predict the future use of books at least as well as any other method known to us.

The objective system seems to agree with the consensus of a group of scholars....[71]

In one sense, Fussler and Simon's entire study was a validation. A prediction was made based on the use patterns prior to 1954, and the period of 1954 to 1958 was then checked to validate the prediction.

5. **Trueswell, Richard William.** Trueswell has published five works[72] that are significant. In his dissertation,[73] he approached the weeding problem from the point of view of its applicability to data processing and computer techniques. The study consisted basically of a number of questionnaires used to determine the "behavioral patterns and requirements of users of a large university library system."[74] As a reinforcing effort, "samples of current circulation were made to determine circulation rates, charge date distributions, and book age distributions."[75] It was this offshoot of the main research that was of most interest.

The basic purpose of this part of the study was to identify a core collection. It was an assumption of Trueswell, gathered from the literature, that "only a very small portion of the library's holdings are in circulation very frequently."[76] He described this sub-set of volumes as the "core" and defined the term "core collection" as a percentage of the collection that should satisfy a given level of the user circulation requirements.[77]

His methodology was to examine the books currently circulating and to analyze them in terms of two variables: " ... one in terms of book age and one in terms of the previous time that the book had been in circulation."[78] Concerning the present circulation, he maintained that it is reasonable to assume that the " ... frequency distribution of the circulation is representative of future circulation.... "[79]

Another facet of Trueswell's discussion was determining an acceptable percentage for the circulation need unsatisfied by a core collection.[80] He suggested that perhaps 1 percent or less would be a desirable figure. His methodology attempted to create core collections at this level. His major findings were:

... approximately one-fourth of the current holdings in the Technical Institute Library should satisfy over 99 percent of the requirements for circulation.[81]

and that at Deering:

... 20% of the present holding could be expected to satisfy over 99% of the circulation requirements.[82]

Further, that:

> The core collection concept can be extended further for use as a tool to thin out the current holdings of the library. Analysis of circulation patterns reveals that over 99% of the current circulation activity is from a population of books each of which has been loaned at least once during the past 18 years for the Deering Library and the past 8 years for the Tech Library.[83]

In his second work,[84] Trueswell dealt with a strategy for weeding employing user needs as a criterion. Again he used "last circulation date" as a circulation predictor. He began by stating that he did not advocate "the arbitrary thinning and discarding of books from a library" and that the decision to do so is a policy decision that must be made by the administration of the library. Nevertheless, a major problem of libraries is how to cope with the increasing size of their holdings. Because periodicals are not very likely targets for thinning, the focus was on monographs. Among Trueswell's conclusions were the following:

> It is suggested that the criteria for stack thinning should be designed to help the library satisfy the requirements of the users of the library.[85]

> This statistic [age of the volume], when translated into the percentage of holdings satisfying a given percentage of circulation, does not lead itself to thinning of monographs.[86]

Also the relevanct was his clear-cut explanation of "cut-off date":

> We now have a way to remove books from the stacks by using the following decision rule: Remove all books that have not circulated during the previous eight year peirod.[87]

In Trueswell's next significant contribution,[88] he combined most of the information and opinion found in his two previous works, using the article to restate the reaffirm his findings. Here has been found the strongest statement as to the meaning of his findings.

> With this approach we are in effect saying that there is a predictable optimal number of volumes for a library's core collection that will satisfy a given percent of user circulation requirements.[89]

> It appears that the last circulation date may be an ideal statistic to define and measure circulation requirements and patterns.[90]

> It is possible that the last circulation date statistic could serve as a tool or a guide to assist the librarian in the stack thinning or weeding process.[91]

> A rather general assumption made in this approach is that the circulation pattern as measured today is typical of the circulation pattern of five, ten, or twelve years in the past. This may not be an unreasonable assumption based on the original and subsequent data.[92]

In another article by Trueswell,[93] some new data were presented. The author studied two libraries not previously reported upon. These were the Mount Holyoke College Library and the Goodell Library, University of Massachusetts. The data from these libraries were compared with the Deering Library data. His conclusions were that "the experience of these three libraries proved to be surprisingly similar."[94] He also suggested, for the first time, that this technique should have application in "circulation-oriented public libraries."[95]

His fresh approach toward identifying a core collection might have some practical use for libraries without adequate circulation records.

> We, therefore, go back x years and starting at that point in time, we adopt in our model the procedure of placing a red X on the cover of each book borrowed. As time progresses, more and more of the books borrowed will have a red X on the cover. After several years, we will reach a point where ninety-nine percent of the books brought to the desk for circulation will already have red X's.[96]

At this point, the core collection would consist of all having the red X.

Trueswell's last work[97] was more detailed than his earlier journal articles. In it he recommended the employment of:

> ... the last circulation date as a statistic to help describe library user circulation requirements.[98]

This would determine what to hold and what to weed. He reported, in greater detail, on the same libraries dealt with before—Mount Holyoke, Goodell, and Forbes (Public) Library. He added a warning that:

> It is extremely important that circulation systems incorporate procedures that will record in some way the date [of the circulations]....[99]

Trueswell recommended that a further use of this data could help decide which titles should be acquired in multiple copies. While no clear-cut decision rule was given, it was suggested that volumes having the most recent circulation dates be considered first when ordering duplicating copies.

In an expanded approach, he emphasized that this method of tallying cumulative distribution functions of last circulation dates gives one a simple decision role that "allows a quantitative approach to an otherwise subjectively treated phenomena."[100] As such, it not only helps identify candidates for weeding, but it predicts the actual size of the core collection and the effect that weeding will have on future circulation. He again stated that:

> ... there is a group of books that could be called a core collection that circulates quite frequently and that only a very small percentage of circulation represents books that have not circulated within a relatively short time period.[101]

6. **Slote, Stanley J.** This author conducted three serious research studies: the *Five Libraries Study* in 1969;[102] the Harrison Public Library Study in 1973;[103] and the Larchmont Public Library Study in 1980.[104] The *Five Libraries Study* dealt only with adult fiction collections. The Harrison Study involved weeding the adult fiction and biography collections but gathered data on the entire library collection. The Larchmont Study included the entire adult collection.

The three objectives of the *Five Libraries Study* were:

1. To determine if certain variables could be utilized to create meaningful weeding criteria. In each of five public libraries, two such variables were studied in depth and evaluated. These variables were the "shelf-time period," the time a book remains on the shelf between successive uses; and the age of a book as indicated by the

most recent date printed on the title page or its verso, called "imprint age."

2. To compare the two criteria to determine which was a "better" criterion, that is, which would yield a smaller core collection that would satisfy a given level of predicted future use.

3. To determine if the pattern of use of the volumes currently in circulation (books actually out of the library at the time of the study) was as valid a predictor of future use as are historical reconstructions of usage over much longer periods of time.

The basic findings of this study were:

1. Past use patterns, as described by shelf-time period, are highly predictive of the future use, and can be used to create meaningful weeding criteria.[105]

2. The "imprint age" is a weaker predictor of future use than "shelf-time period."

3. The "shelf-time period" is a predictor of a "better" core collection than the "most recent imprint date" because it describes a smaller core collection for the same level of predicted future use. From a practical point of view, the difference was so significant that the "imprint date" should not be considered as a useful weeding criterion.[106]

4. That each library tends to have its own unique patterns of circulation, and each needs to be studied individually.[107] No method was found to apply the information developed in one library as a weeding criterion for another library.

5. That the "current circulation" method creates shelf-time period patterns that are as valid for predicting future use as is the method of historical reconstruction.[108]

6. That shelf-time period patterns predict future use patterns.[109] A return to Tarrytown seven weeks after predicting the use to be made of the core collection showed such a prediction to have been accurate.

The study of the Harrison Public Library was an attempt to put into practice the theoretical findings of the earlier study, in which no actual weeding had taken place. The adult fiction and biography collections were weeded, using the Spine-Marking Method (see p. 122). The goals of this study were:

1. To validate the theory of weeding by use of the shelf-time period criterion. A prediction was made about the impact weeding would have on future circulation, and such prediction was checked periodically after the weeding had been completed.

2. To discover if in one library different classes of books varied in their shelf-time period patterns.

3. To validate the Spine-Marking Method of weeding. This is the first time a library was weeded exclusively by this method, and a study was made of its value as a practical weeding technique.

The major findings were:

1. When shelf-time period was used as the weeding criterion, the amount of circulation was not reduced by the removal of a substantial number of volumes from the collection.[110] This was the most unexpected result of the study. Although it had been predicted that only 96 percent of the former fiction circulation would be retained, in fact, circulation increased. Six months after removing approximately 20 percent of the volumes from the collection, the circulation increased to 106.2 percent of previous circulation; and 20 months later it increased to 121.2 percent.[111] This was in a library where the rest of the collection enjoyed no increase in circulation. In the biography collection, with almost 50 percent of the volumes removed from the shelves, circulation remained constant. Weeding the collections seemed to increase usage, not reduce it, as predicted.

2. There were substantial differences in shelf-time periods among the various classes of books.[112] Tables 5 and 6 (pages 82 and 83) reflect these differences, in a number of arbitrarily selected classes.

3. The library's holdings in the various classes were not in proportion to the use being made of those classes.[113] Table 4, below, illustrates this characteristic:

Table 4
PERCENTAGE OF USE VERSUS PERCENTAGE OF HOLDINGS, HARRISON, ADULT COLLECTION

Adult Collection

Class	Percentage of Circulation Represented by This Class	Percentage of the Library's Holdings Represented by This Class
Fiction	48.2	25.8
Paperbacks	6.5	3.0
Biography	3.4	5.5
Non-Fiction-Other	41.9	65.7
Total	100.0%	100.0%

Children's Collection

Fiction	45.5	40.1
Picture Books	25.8	11.9
Biography	2.6	5.2
Non-Fiction-Other	26.1	42.8
Total	100.0%	100.0%

Table 5

SHELF-TIME PERIODS OF THE CIRCULATION AND COLLECTION SAMPLES COMPARED (%), HARRISON, ADULT SECTION

Cumulative Shelf-Time Period	Fiction		Paperbacks		Biography		Non-Fiction 000–999+		Total	
	Circula-tion	Collec-tion	Circula-tion	Collec-tion	Circula-tion	Collec-tion	Circula-tion	Collec-tion	Circula-tion	Collec-tion
0	49	29	–	29	–	8	47	13	50	17
1	78	42	68	26	67	14	60	21	70	26
2	97	51	77	35	100	17	72	26	83	32
3	84	57	64	45	62	20	69	29	75	36
4	86	63	73	54	75	23	66	35	76	42
5	76	75	88	63	86	30	77	43	78	52
6	96	78	90	63	100	27	83	47	90	54
7	95	80	63	69	79	36	74	51	83	59
8	96	84	85	73	75	43	82	53	87	61
9	95	85	90	64	88	42	84	57	90	63
10	99*	93	77	68	81	44	77	59	86	69
11	99	93	87	71	92	46	93	61	96	73
12	98	93	84	69	90	42	89	60	94	72
13	99	95	91	74	91	61	92	69	96	80
14	98	–	80	–	91	–	90	–	93	–
15	99	–	91	–	91	–	90	–	94	–

*Collection weeded.

Table 6

SHELF-TIME PERIODS OF THE CIRCULATION AND COLLECTION SAMPLES COMPARED (%), HARRISON, CHILDREN'S SECTION

Cumulative Shelf-Time Period	Fiction		Picture Books		Biography		Non-Fiction		Total	
	Circula-tion	Collec-tion	Circula-tion	Collec-tion	Circula-tion	Collec-tion	Circula-tion	Collec-tion	Circula-tion	Collec-tion
0	62	33	61	61	43	8	39	17	58	28
1	81	37	63	78	–	12	68	23	75	23
2	84	46	71	78	–	14	80	27	76	29
3	81	51	87	83	14	17	58	29	75	33
4	77	54	71	86	100	20	59	35	70	37
5	90	56	89	90	63	22	49	37	73	40
6	85	58	94	95	100	26	73	47	86	48
7	88	60	95	95	52	30	75	48	84	49
8	91	61	95	89	50	39	79	49	88	49
9	90	68	100	89	71	42	91	55	91	53
10	85	70	90	89	43	48	86	57	84	55
11	90	69	92	81	–	49	81	59	88	55
12	90	75	90	88	60	49	88	59	88	57
13	92	77	86	–	83	54	90	65	90	61
14	97	–	100	–	62	–	89	–	96	–
15	100	–	100	–	71	–	91	–	96	–

For example, although 25 percent of the Harrison adult holdings were fiction, 48 percent of the adult usage was fiction. It was hypothesized that an idealized collection, optimizing book investment, should hold classes of books in proportion to their usage. A "better collection" would have 48 percent of the collection experiencing 48 percent of the use.

4. Substantial monthly pulsations of circulation patterns called for caution in making the final weeding decision too rapidly or with too few samples.[114] Table 5, page 82, shows these fluctuations. The fiction sample, which had at least 200 cases each month, had the least fluctuation. The other classes had relatively few samples per month, sometimes as few as 5. It is recommended that for any class being weeded, the weeding decision be made from a sample of at least 400 cases.

5. Non-core volumes, retained because of professional judgment, should have been weeded.[115]

6. The Spine-Marking Method of weeding is a valid and useful method, but needs to be applied with care.[116]

The Larchmont Library Study was made to compare the "current circulation method" of creating shelf-time periods, from a sample of the most recent week's usage, with the "historical reconstruction method," which creates shelf-time periods from a sample of 10 years' usage. This study showed that at levels likely to be used for weeding, no significant differences could be detected (see p. 121). It confirmed again the likelihood that usage patterns do not change over extended periods of time.

7. **Urquhart, J. A., and Urquhart, N. C.** The Urquharts have produced a book[117] representing several studies undertaken by C. R. Taylor, B. J. Enright, and themselves at the Newcastle upon Tyne University. The two-year research project attempted to design and evaluate "procedures for selecting items for suitable relegation" which would have general applicability to other university libraries. They accepted the use of the last circulation date after studying the serious literature in the field. Among their more interesting findings were:

1. "Cost of relegation must be allowed for as a regular item in the library budget.... Eventually the amount of relegation must rise to approach the rate of acquisition."[118]

2. "Recently acquired stock is what is most used in academic libraries. These become eventual candidates for relegation."[119]

3. "Relegation of periodicals can be based on borrowing data.... "[120]

4. There is not a significant difference between subjects when not more than 1 or 2 percent of current borrowings should be affected (by weeding). "A uniform decision can be applied over the whole stock."[121]

These studies leaned heavily on previous research and are an example of cumulative research creating cumulative knowledge. They also highlight for the first time two important concepts rarely found in the literature:

1. That weeding (relegation) must become a standard, normal, properly supported routine, equal in many ways to the efforts involved in library acquisitions.

2. That the differences in circulation patterns found in different subject areas were not significant enough to prevent the use of a uniform cut-point for all subjects involved in a single library.

8. **Kent, Allen, and others.** The University of Pittsburgh Study[122] took place over a period exceeding seven years. It recorded the acquisitions made from October 1968 through 1975 and observed the use made of these acquisitions as time passed. According to this report, materials should be "both useful and used." A goal of the research was to develop measures for determining the extent to which library materials are used and when materials should be purged from the collections.

Among the findings were that:

1. " ... a minority of titles accounts for a majority of uses.... "[123]

2. Books and journals are subject to rapid rates of aging and obselescence.[124]

3. 39.8 percent of the books acquired in 1969 never circulated during the first six years on the library's shelves.[125]

4. There is no objective way to make acquisition decisions with certain knowledge that what is acquired will be used.[126]

5. " ... external circulation data can be utilized with a high level of confidence to measure total book use.... "[127]

6. " ... random samples of loan records representing as few as three days produced correlations as high as .95 with total population in regard to present circulation use.... "[128] One does not need long-term data to predict future use.

7. 48.37 percent of the total collection did not circulate in seven years.[129]

8. A definite aging pattern emerges.[130] As books get older, first-time use is reduced. For example, for 36,869 books acquired in 1969:[131]

Year	# First Circulated
1969	9,708
1970	6,424
1971	2,449
1972	1,452
1973	915
1974	644
1975	580

9. " ... each year's acquisitions behave much like any other year."[132]

10. Only objective techniques of weeding should be used.[133]

11. " ... past use is the best indicator of the future use of material."[134]

REFERENCES

1. Aridaman K. Jain and others, "A Statistical Study of Book Use Supplemented with a Bibliography of Library Use Studies" (unpublished Ph.D. dissertation, Purdue University, 1967).

2. Charles H. Busha and Royal Purcell, "A Textural Approach for Promoting Rigorous Research in Librarianship," *Journal of Education for Librarianship* XIV (Summer 1973), p. 3.

3. Charles William Eliot, "The Division of a Library into Books in Use, and Books Not in Use, with Different Storage Methods for the Two Classes of Books," *Library Journal* XXVII (July 1902), pp. 51-56.

4. Ibid., p. 52.

5. Ibid.

6. Ibid.

7. Samuel H. Ranck, "The Problem of the Unused Book," *Library Journal* XXXVI (August 1911), pp. 428-29.

8. Ibid., p. 428.

9. Ibid., p. 429.

10. Lee Ash, *Yale's Selective Book Retirement Program* (Hamden, CT: Archon Books, 1963).

11. Ibid., p. 81.

12. Ibid., p. x.

13. Ibid., p. 28.

14. Ibid., p. 52.

15. Ralph E. Ellsworth, *The Economics of Book Storage in College and University Libraries* (Washington: Association of Research, 1969).

16. Ash, *Yale's Selective Book Retirement Program*, pp. 66-67.

17. Elizabeth Mueller, "Are New Books Read More Than Old Ones?" *Library Quarterly* XXXV (July 1965), pp. 166-72.

18. M. K. Buckland and others, *Systems Analysis of a University Library* (Lancaster: University of Lancaster Library Occasional Papers No. 4, 1970), p. 1.

19. Ibid.

20. S. C. Bradford, "Sources of Information of Specific Subjects," *Engineering* CXXXVII (January 26, 1934), pp. 85-86.

21. Buckland, *Systems Analysis of a University Library*, p. 8.

22. Ibid., p. 10.

23. Ibid., p. 12.

24. Ibid.

25. Ibid., p. 52.

26. Ibid., p. 53.

27.   Philip M. Morse, *Library Effectiveness: A Systems Approach* (Cambridge, MA: M.I.T. Press, 1968).

28.   Ibid., p. 1.

29.   Ibid., p. 5.

30.   Ibid., p. 83.

31.   Ibid., pp. 83-84.

32.   Ibid., p. 93.

33.   Ibid., pp. 167-68.

34.   Ibid., p. 168.

35.   Stanley J. Slote, "An Approach to Weeding Criteria for Newspaper Libraries," *American Documentation* XIX (April 1968), pp. 168-72.

36.   In the *Five Libraries Study*, much material was excluded from the sample because no data was available on the book card. It was felt that often this was because the material had never been used. Such observation led to the suggestion that all book cards be *dated* when placed into books.

37.   Elmer M. Grieder, "The Effect of Book Storage on Circulation Service," *College and Research Libraries* XI (October 1950), pp. 374-76.

38.   This technique may have the weakness that books in the hands of the clients at any one moment may not represent the true circulation pattern. Certain types of books may be returned more rapidly than others, and then recirculated. For instance, if 1,000 fiction volumes and 1,000 non-fiction were in circulation at one time, and fiction was kept out for 10 days on an average while non-fiction was retained for 20 days, fiction would be under-represented by 50 percent in the sample.

39.   Marianne Cooper, "Criteria for Weeding of Collections," *Library Resources and Technical Services* XII (Summer 1968), pp. 339-51.

40.   Ibid., p. 349.

41.   Charles F. Gosnell, "Obsolescence of Books in College Libraries," *College and Research Libraries* V (March 1944), pp. 115-25.

42.   Lloyd J. Houser, *New Jersey Area Libraries: A Pilot Project toward the Evaluation of the Reference Collection* (New Brunswick, NJ: New Jersey Library Association, 1968).

43.   Ibid., pp. 30-31. In this quotation, there have been omitted some of the specific references to the type of collection and volumes Houser was studying in order to relate these statements more closely to the present study.

44.   Winston Charles Lister, "Least Cost Decision Rules for the Selection of Library Materials for Compact Storage" (unpublished Ph.D. dissertation, Purdue University, 1967).

45.   Ibid., p. 12.

46.   Ibid., p. 6.

47.   Ibid., p. 223.

48.   Ibid., p. 226.

49.   Ibid., p. 224.

50.   Ibid., p. 223.

51.   Ibid., p. 103.

52.   Ibid., p. 116.

53.   Ibid., p. 115.

54.   Edward A. Silver, "A Quantitative Appraisal of the M.I.T. Science Library Mezzanine with an Application to the Problem of Limited Shelf Space" (unpublished term paper for M.I.T. graduate course 8:75, Operations Research, 1962).

55.   Ibid., p. 2.

56.   Ibid., p. 50.

57.   A. K. Jain, "Sampling and Short-Period Usage in the Purdue Library," *College and Research Libraries* XXVII (May 1966), pp. 211-18.

58.   Jain, "A Statistical Study of Book Use...."

59.   Ibid., pp. 128-220.

60.   Ibid., p. 125.

61.   Herman H. Fussler and Julian L. Simon, *Patterns in the Use of Books in Large Research Libraries* (Chicago: University of Chicago Press, 1969).

62.   Ibid., p. 2.

63.   Ibid., p. 7.

64.   Ibid., pp. 45, 52.

65.   Ibid., p. 30.

66.   Ibid., p. 31.

67.   Ibid., p. 15.

68.   Ibid., p. 144.

69.   Ibid., pp. 66-67.

70.   Ibid., p. 143.

71.   Ibid., p. 147.

72.   See bibliography for full citations of the five works.

73.   Richard William Trueswell, "User Behavioral Patterns and Requirements and Their Effect on the Possible Applications of Data Processing and Computer Techniques in a University Library" (unpublished Ph.D. dissertation, Northwestern University, 1964).

74.   Ibid., p. iv.

75.   Ibid.

76.   Ibid., p. 35.

77.   Ibid., pp. 109-116.

78.   Ibid., p. 44.

79.   Ibid., p. 105.

80. Ibid., p. 112.

81. Ibid., p. 113.

82. Ibid.

83. Ibid., p. 180.

84. Richard W. Trueswell, "A Quantitative Measure of User Circulation Requirements and Its Possible Effect on Stack Thinning and Multiple Copy Determination," *American Documentation* XVI (January 1965), pp. 20-25.

85. Ibid., p. 22.

86. Ibid.

87. Ibid.

88. Richard W. Trueswell, "Determining the Optimal Number of Volumes for a Library's Core Collection," *Libri* XVI (1966), pp. 49-60.

89. Ibid., p. 58.

90. Ibid., p. 59.

91. Ibid.

92. Ibid., p. 57.

93. Richard W. Trueswell, "User Circulation Satisfaction vs. Size of Holdings at Three Academic Libraries," *College and Research Libraries* XXX (May 1969), pp. 204-213.

94. Ibid., p. 204.

95. Trueswell, "Determining the Optimal Number of Volumes for a Library's Core Collection," p. 49.

96. Ibid., p. 52.

97. Richard W. Trueswell, *Analysis of Library User Circulation Requirements* (Amherst: University of Massachusetts, 1968).

98. Ibid., abstract.

99. Ibid., pp. 2-3.

100. Ibid., p. 22.

101. Ibid., p. 7.

102. Stanley J. Slote, *Weeding Library Collections* (Littleton, CO: Libraries Unlimited, 1975).

103. Ibid.

104. Stanley J. Slote (unpublished study).

105. Slote, *Weeding Library Collections*, p. 81.

106. Ibid., p. 82.

107. Ibid.

108. Ibid.

109. Ibid., pp. 81-82.

110. Ibid., p. 86.

111. M. Poller, "Weeding Monographs in the Harrison Public Library," *The De-acquisitions Librarian* I (Spring 1976), p. 7. Reprinted in full, p. 179 of this book.

112. Slote, *Weeding Library Collections*, pp. 81, 87, 88.

113. Ibid., p. 93.

114. Ibid., p. 86.

115. Ibid., p. 93.

116. Ibid., p. 86.

117. J. A. Urquhart and N. C. Urquhart, *Relegation and Stock Control in Libraries* (Boston: Oriel Press, 1976).

118. Ibid., p. 37.

119. Ibid.

120. Ibid., p. 38.

121. Ibid., p. 86.

122. Allen Kent and others, *Use of Library Materials: The University of Pittsburgh Study* (New York: Marcel Dekker, 1979).

123. Ibid., p. 2.

124. Ibid.

125. Ibid., p. 9.

126. Ibid., p. 2.

127. Ibid., p. 10.

128. Ibid.

129. Ibid., p. 13.

130. Ibid., pp. 13-14.

131. Ibid., p. 14.

132. Ibid., p. 19.

133. Ibid., p. 48.

134. Ibid., p. 49.

PART 2
The Weeding Process

9

THE NEW CONCEPT IN WEEDING

BACKGROUND

For hundreds of years library weeding has been accomplished by the subjective application of vague rules, concepts, or feelings—difficult to describe accurately, difficult to apply with consistency, and difficult to measure as to their validity. This book discourages the use of this approach, an approach that lacks the ability to predict which volumes are likely to enjoy future usage and which are not. The result is that many useful works are discarded and many useless ones are retained. To replace this method, the author searched for, found, and studied a simple variable that could predict future usage with certainty. This variable was based upon past or current usage patterns observed in the library. During the last 20 years, other possible variables have been studied and rejected as lacking practical, efficient predictive strength. These discarded variables have included the age of the volumes, the language used, the subject matter, and the type of work.

A WEEDING VARIABLE

The nature of the desired variable can be best understood by reducing the concept to absurdity. Suppose, for instance, it was discovered in a specific library that only volumes with green bindings were used. No book (regardless of subject, title, author, age, or location) was used if it did not have a green binding. If the library then removed all volumes which lacked green bindings, theoretically, the usage of that library would remain unaffected. There would now be left in the library a subset of volumes which could be described or defined by the simple variable: "green bindings." This subset or "core collection" would satisfy 100 percent of all future demands made upon this library.

In this example, one could say that a variable has been identified which predicts with confidence the subset of volumes which experience 100 percent of all the usage. (This assumes that no short-term event or condition has caused exclusive use of green bound volumes.) Library usage would not be reduced by the removal of the non-green volumes. A variable has been identified which predicts the future usage of the library. Of course, this example is foolish, as no such situation was ever encountered, nor is it likely to be encountered. However, it points up the concept involved in searching for a variable that could describe the current library usage.

SHELF-TIME PERIOD AS A VARIABLE

As this book has stated, a variable has been uncovered, studied, applied, and found to be of value in solving the weeding problem. This strong, valid, positive, predictive, meaningful variable is called *shelf-time period*. Shelf-time period is the length of time a book remains on the shelf between circulations. For practical purposes, it may also be considered an open-ended period, reflecting the time that has passed between the previous usage of a book and the day weeding is being done. In this case, the open-end shelf-time period measures a period still ongoing, and therefore it measures period of time *no less* than the next true shelf-time period would have been if the volume had been given the opportunity to be used again.

To better understand the concept and use of the shelf-time period, replace the variable "green bindings" with the variable "one year shelf-time period." Suppose that in a library, every volume which was used during the entire history of the library had remained on the shelf less than one year since its previous use or its acquisition. This means that 100 percent of the usage had a shelf-time period of under one year. If one then removes from the library shelves all the volumes which have remained on the shelves unused for one year or more, one would have removed books which will not circulate in the future. The result would be a core collection that would likely retain 100 percent of the future use of the library.

Theoretically, past use is not an absolute predictor of future use. But practically, in library after library where the assumption of predictability has been tested, it has been shown that past use had been a reliable, valid predictor of future use. Furthermore, in *every* case where shelf-time period has been used for weeding, contrary to expectations, *usage was found to increase* (see p. 81). Thus, this variable as a predictor of future use can be applied without fear of reducing the value of the collection.

Intuitively, most librarians can accept the principles being advanced above. For example, if advised to remove all volumes which have experienced no usage in 20 years, few would resist this advice. If a book hasn't been used in the last 20 years it seems unlikely that it will be used in the next 20 years. However, as the time span is reduced, resistance to weeding is increased. A few librarians would resist if asked to remove volumes not used for 10 years; and even more would resist 5 years. Under the methods to be described shortly, the cut-point is frequently 2 or 3 years; and sometimes it is as little as 1 year. And here massive resistance is likely unless librarians understand the underlying concepts.

Once agreeing to the principle, it is necessary to measure the shelf-time periods of volumes in use and try to predict what will happen when books are removed from the shelves based upon such measurements. The following three chapters deal in detail with the processes used to weed a library without fear of depriving the clients or harming the collection.

THE CORE COLLECTION

Another concept is integral to the understanding of this approach to weeding. Through our studies it has been found that: *every library consists of two distinguishable collections, the collection that is used and the collection that remains in the library unused.* These two collections are not apparent to the naked eye, even to the experienced eye of a well-trained librarian. The collections look alike. Each subset consists of newer volumes and older ones, of all subjects, and frequently one author has volumes in both collections. These subsets are called the *core collection* and the *non-core collection*. The core collection is a subset of holdings which should be retained by the library for its clients' use, and the non-core collection is that subset representing little or no usage and should be considered for weeding. The problem to be dealt with is how to identify these two sub-collections with confidence and certainty.

Once these two collections are identified, the following rules should be followed:

No volume in the core collection should be considered for weeding.

As a corollary of the above rule:

All books in the non-core collection are candidates for weeding, and probably should be weeded.

It has been observed that librarians studying the non-core collection frequently identify volumes they are reluctant to remove from the primary holding areas. The reasons are many: these volumes may have been gifts from powerful trustees, or local authors; works may be related to local history; or works may be by very famous authors. Such volumes and others librarians identify for keeping may be retained, although they will not experience much use. They become permanent shelf-sitters and will show up again during the next weeding effort as belonging to the non-core collection. So keep whatever your judgment dictates. If done in moderation, retaining non-core volumes in the core collection will not subvert the beneficial effects of weeding.

PATTERNS OF USE

Almost all of the recent studies in book use have re-enforced the needs and pressures for weeding. Some even question present techniques of book acquisition. Perhaps no study is more shocking and important than that at the University of Pittsburgh, which found that *40 percent of all books purchased by the university library are never used* (see p. 85). This means that newly purchased books frequently enter the non-core collection immediately and never serve any practical purpose as far as the library client is concerned. The removal of these volumes would have no known negative effect. This present work does not address the problem of preventing this terrible waste. Unfortunately, weeding attacks the problem after the fact. It would be extremely valuable if a predictor could be discovered to identify, in advance, volumes that will never be used, but to date no such predictor has been uncovered or reported in the literature. By using the methods that follow, such volumes will be weeded from the collection after the user has cast his vote on their value by permitting them to remain unused on the library shelves.

It would be unfair to conclude that all kinds of libraries suffer from the same problem. The purchase of useless books is mainly a problem for research, university, college, and special libraries; it has not been a problem in most public libraries or in school libraries. A major finding of our studies is that in middle-sized and smaller public libraries, practically all new books enjoy use while they are relatively new. In studying the fiction collections of seven public libraries, this author found *no case of a new book remaining on the shelf unused during the first two years after its acquisition and shelving.* To put it another way, in these libraries all fiction volumes, when first acquired, became part of the core collection.

THE CORE COLLECTION CHANGES

The above pattern of book use in a public library is well known to working librarians. New books, especially best-sellers, are in tremendous demand while they remain in the public eye. The library is able to satisfy only a small part of the demand, numerous reservation cards are filed, and the book is never found on the shelf during this period. Then usage generally tapers off a little, and in a year or two circulation either stops all together or becomes sporadic. Some volumes taper off more slowly and may receive substantial use for 5, 10, or even 20 years. Ultimately, all but a handful of books (which from the point of view of use might be considered "the classics") move into the non-core collection and get little or no use. It is for this reason that weeding is a never-ending process.

As can be seen, the core and non-core collections in active libraries are in a constant state of flux, with all but a tiny amount of the movement being from the core to the non-core collection. A new book is received and shelved. It receives rather heavy usage for a time, and then the rate of usage is reduced rather steadily. Finally, unless it is a classic, all or most usage stops. On the other hand, a counter trend also exists. Authors and titles occasionally are revived. This is particularly true if a movie or TV persentation generates new interest in a work. And so on rare occasions volumes move from the non-core back to the core collection. This means that at any time there is some usage of the non-core collection and some non-usage of the core collection. *Under any method of weeding, it is likely that some books which are removed might have been used if they had not been weeded.*

EFFECTS OF WEEDING

In using the methods recommended in this book, weeding is frequently done at the *96 percent keeping level.* That is to say that theoretically the core collection retained after weeding will retain 96 percent of the collection's former use. The non-core collection, now weeded, therefore represented 4 percent of the usage. In the field it was observed that, generally, between 10 and 50 percent of the collection could be weeded out at this keeping level; and that 50 to 90 percent of the collection (the remainder) represented 96 percent of the use. This *is* only theoretical, for *in every case where libraries were weeded the book use (as reflected by the circulation count) either stayed the same or increased.* Thus, while some books that would have been used have been removed, the general appearance, quality, and tone of the remaining books seem to encourage more rather than less use. In reality, at no substantial cost, the library has been enlarged by making room for more new books, and active usage of the existing collection has been increased. This is the best of both worlds, for now fewer books create more usage.

PROCEDURES WHICH REDUCE THE
CORE COLLECTION UNINTENTIONALLY

Book-use studies have uncovered two library procedures which reduce the use that new volumes would normally have experienced. Such procedures make rational weeding procedures less effective.

First, as mentioned above, as new books start to age they tend to lose their client appeal. It was observed that some libraries catalog new acquisitions so slowly, that on an average they take between one year and 18 months to reach the stacks. The quickest and most satisfying way to increase library usage is to get new books on the shelves immediately upon their receipt, even if complete cataloging must be deferred. The presence of a volume on the shelf is vastly more important to its future use than the precision of its cataloging. The slowdown in processing frequently destroys any reader interest that might have existed earlier. Books become automatic members of the non-core collection and candidates for weeding through this delay. No library practice could be more destructive to the normal use patterns.

Second, and perhaps less forgivable, is the practice of librarians storing new books in their own offices or homes for future reading, before these books have been made available to the clients. In one small library, it was observed that over 150 new or practically new volumes were being kept in the head librarian's office waiting to be read before being shelved. The tendency to put off the actual reading (sometimes permanently) often causes a core book to be moved to the non-core collection. To prevent this destructive practice, all librarians should be subject to the same circulation rules as their patrons.

RETAINING THE CORE COLLECTION

All of the recommended methods of weeding work the same way. They analyze the book use in terms of shelf-time period. Having analyzed the use pattern, such data is quantified. This tabulation then creates a *cut-point* so that the entire collection can be altered in such a fashion that only the core collection is retained in the primary storage areas (the stacks).

The methods are based upon the realization that all volumes currently circulating (or enjoying in-library use) are part of the core collection. By measuring the shelf-time periods of the volumes being used, the methods create a specific date to be used as a cut-point. It might be concluded, for example, that all volumes not used since December 4, 1980 are to be weeded and that the core collection consists of all volumes used at least once since that date. Where a date is not stated as such in the result (as in the Spine-Marking Method), it, in fact, still exists.

SAMPLING TO DETERMINE THE CUT-POINT

All the methods about to be described call for no fewer than 400 useful samples. This number has a solid statistical basis. For practical purposes, it is wise to collect 500 samples so that useless samples can be discarded and at least 400 meaningful uses are available for the tabulations.

IN-LIBRARY USE

The methods recommended tend to focus on measuring the shelf-time periods of books that circulate, since such relevant data is either available or easy to create. The cut-date determined for the circulating collection can be used safely for that collection even if the collection also receives in-library use. It has been found in several serious studies that in-library usage of a collection is substantially the same as the circulation usage.

But part of a library's usage is in house, frequently of volumes that do not circulate. This usage can be from reserved collections; from reference collections; from non-circulating non-book materials (periodicals, records, etc.); and from works used only by the librarians, such as ready-reference works and cataloging tools. Such works should be weeded independently of the circulating collection.

To weed these collections properly, a technique must be utilized to record in-library usage. Clients must be prevented from shelving works they have removed from the shelves. Clerks should reshelve these works, marking them properly first. Librarians should mark each volume they use in the library. Reserved collections must have charge-out systems compatible with the needs of the weeding method being used. The Spine-Marking Method can be used effectively for in-library use, even if another method is used to weed the circulating collection.

RECOMMENDED WEEDING METHODS

There are five valid methods for developing the kind of weeding criteria recommended in this book. The practical choice depends upon the information which is readily available or can be made available conveniently. These are:

1. The Book Card Method (p. 101)
   a. The Substitute Book Card Method (p. 116)
2. The Spine-Marking Method (p. 122)
3. The Historical Reconstruction Method (p. 142)
4. The Computer Method (p. 99)
5. The Substitute Spine-Marking Method (p. 141)
   a. The Machine Charging Method
   b. The Fortuitous Indication Method

HOW TO SELECT THE BEST WEEDING METHOD

The best method for weeding a circulating library depends upon the system of circulation control being used. Four major systems of circulation control are in general use. However, in each method, the completeness of the data available and the ability to use such data are of prime importance in determining the weeding method. From the point of view of circulation control systems, here is a guide for the selection of the proper weeding method.

1. **The Book Card System of Circulation Control.** In this system, a book card remains in the book when on the shelves, is removed at the circulation

station when the book is circulated, and the card is stamped with a due date. The book card is then filed at the circulation desk, usually by due date, and is re-slipped into the book when the book is returned to the library and discharged.

If the book card contains the complete due date, including the YEAR, use the Book Card Method of weeding.

If the rate of book use is so slow that it would take too long (months or years) to accumulate 400 samples at the circulation station, use the Historical Reconstruction Method. This method is particularly useful when only one small class of books is to be weeded.

If the due date indication lacks the YEAR, use the Spine-Marking Method.

If the current circulation stations or records are not available to the weeders, use the Historical Reconstruction Method. Such a case would be a central library which supplies branches with books but has no circulation of its own.

If the due date indication lacks the YEAR, but is color-coded so that the year of use can be reconstructed, use the Substitute Book Card Method.

2. **The Transaction Card System of Circulation Control.** This system includes most photographic and computer systems. Under this system, the book cards remain permanently in the book and are not marked with a due date. The book information is recorded on a transaction card and on the user identification card. The due date is shown on the transaction card, which is slipped into the book pocket when the book is charged out. When the book is returned, the transaction card is removed and its transaction number tabulated. If any successive number in a run is missing, it is looked up on the permanent records (photo or computer) in order to reconstruct the book and client information necessary to undertake the overdue procedures.

If the transaction card system controls the circulation, use the Spine-Marking Method for weeding.

3. **The Charge Slip System of Circulation Control.** This system has the client filling out a preprinted form which records all the information needed: the user, the book information, and the date. These slips are frequently filed by classification number, and used to locate a specific book which has been requested and not found on the shelves. Multiple copies of the form permit other filing runs, such as due date, if deemed useful. This is an older system used mostly in college, research, and university libraries, and its usage is decreasing.

If charge slips control circulation, use the Spine-Marking Method of weeding.

4. **Computer Circulation Control.** Here the information relating to due date, borrower, and the book is machine readable and is recorded by a computer. The book card remains in the book when it circulates. The book is discharged by the computer, which later prints out a list of overdues with the information necessary to remedy the situation.

If the computer is not programmed for weeding, use the Spine-Marking Method for weeding.

If the computer is programmed for weeding, use the Computer Method for weeding. This method involves the computer being programmed to measure the shelf-time periods of all volumes circulating and all volumes on the shelves. It must establish a cut-point and give a print-out of all volumes to be weeded.

Because of its rarity, nothing further will be said in this book about the Computer Method.

5. **Other Circulation Techniques Permitting Weeding.** All of the following accidental or intentional coding of books at the circulation station permit the use of a standard weeding method. If this coding exists, the time lag normally required in some weeding methods can be dramatically reduced and weeding can be accelerated.

A. **Machine Charge Method with dotting (case I).** Certain charging machines are supplied with a little pen tip which can be color-coded. As each book card is machine charged, in addition to its other functions, the machine applies a small dot on the rear of the book card. **If the color-coded dot has been changed yearly, use the Substitute Book Card Method of weeding (p. 116).**

B. **Machine Charge Method with dotting (case II). If a colored dot is applied to the back of the book card, as in case I, but such dot has not been color-coded for each year, use the Substitute Spine-Marking Method (p. 141).** However, this can usually be done where the system was changed to machine charging within the past few years. It can be used *only* when fewer than 96 percent of the book cards being received at the circulation desk to be charged out have been previously dotted.

C. **Color-Coded Due Date Method. If the book card method of circulation control is being used, and the year was omitted from the due date stamp but the color of the ink used for the stamp has been changed yearly, use the Substitute Book Card Method of weeding, "a special case" (p. 117).**

D. **Fortuitous Indication Method.** Occasionally, a change in systems or rules will give an indication useful for weeding. **If in the last few years some addition or omission has been made to volumes when they circulated, use the Substitute Spine-Marking Method (p. 141).** For example, a library was required by state law to start printing on each volume a warning that the stealing of a book was a criminal offense. All books were so stamped as they circulated. Another example is that a new style book card was substituted for an old style card when each book was discharged, after circulating.

10

WHEN TO USE IT

This method can be used only if the following conditions prevail:

1. **That the book card method of circulation control has been used.** It is essential that all the circulating volumes in the library which have been charged out have been date-stamped each time they were circulated. This date might appear either on the book card, on the book pocket, or on a special form permanently attached to the volume.

2. **That all of the dates so stamped contain at least the month and the year.** The absence of the *year* makes this method unusable; the absence of the month might make it unusable.

ADVANTAGES OF THE METHOD

The Book Card Method of weeding is by far the easiest, fastest, and probably the most reliable method of weeding circulating collections. The main advantage of this method is that normally the cut-date can be developed within one hour. In addition, weeding candidates can be selected by non-librarians, since the only expertise required is the ability to read dates. Finally, the library can be weeded rapidly. In the field, it has been found that a motivated worker can examine 200 to 500 volumes per hour, and make the correct weeding decision for each volume.

STEPS TO BE TAKEN BEFORE WEEDING

Step 1: Appoint a weeding manager. Since this entire operation should take only a few days, a senior staff member should be permitted to spend full time organizing and supervising the operation.

Step 2: Organize the entire operation. A complete plan should be created, in writing, covering the following tasks:

A. Establish the date or dates that the actual weeding will take place.

B. Schedule the staff or volunteers who will do the work. A group of 10 assistants is sufficient for most medium-sized libraries.

C. Acquire an adequate number of storage boxes to hold the volumes removed from the stacks. Try to estimate the number needed, figuring that between 10 and 30 percent of the volumes are likely to be removed.

D. Acquire tape or string to secure the packed boxes and marking pencils to note their content.

E. If possible, get one book truck for each worker so that there is a convenient place to put the books as they are removed from the shelves.

F. Schedule a person to physically move the books or boxes from the stack area to storage areas. Maintenance personnel can be used for this purpose.

G. Locate and prepare adequate storage space to hold the books removed from the shelves.

H. Have a half-hour training session with all involved personnel before the weeding starts. (See Instructions for Weeding, which follow.)

I. Announce and publicize the fact that the library will be closed during the weeding period.

J. Schedule a day before the actual weeding for data collection and cut-point determination.

K. Get 3x5-inch cards, two for each shelf involved in the weeding.

L. Get foot stools, tall stools, and short stools so weeders can work sitting down.

Step 3: Test out the system in a trial run. At least one week before the actual weeding, the weeding manager should make a trial run both to create the cut-point and to identify candidates for weeding. This should work out any kinks or doubts in advance.

TRAINING THE WEEDING STAFF

As advised above, a training session should be set up in advance of the actual weeding. It is good practice to have this session immediately prior to the start of weeding. Here is an example of some weeding instructions the author has used several times:

Instructions for Weeding

1. Weed in a fixed order, from top to bottom and from left to right.
2. Place a 3x5-inch card in the middle of a weeded shelf, between two books, clearly visible, to identify that shelf as having been weeded. This is done so that no shelf goes unweeded or none is weeded more than once.

3. The cut-date is _____. (Insert the cut-date determined for your library.) Keep all volumes on the shelf which have been used once or more in _____. (List your cut-date first, then list subsequent years up to the current year. For example, suppose your cut-date is 1976. Fill in the space above: "Keep all volumes on the shelf which have been used once or more in 1977, 1978, 1979, 1980, 1981." The current year should be the last in the sequence.) Place on the book truck all volumes *last used* in the year of the cut-date or earlier. (In the example above, this would be 1976, or earlier.)

4. Many cards have the due dates appearing out of chronological order. Search out the date reflecting the most recent use as the criterion for either leaving a book on the shelf or putting it on the book truck. If a Gaylord charging machine is being used, look at all four possible positions to find the most recent date.

5. If a quick glance at a card indicates any date listed in 3, above (1977, 1978, 1979, 1980, or 1981 in the example), the book is to remain on the shelf. It is then not necessary to search out the most recent date on the book card.

6. If there is any doubt about whether a book should be retained or removed, keep that volume on the shelf.

7. If a book has no due date appearing on the book card, keep that volume if it seems to be a relatively new book or a book that has been given a new book card in the last five years. Remove undated books from the shelf if dusty, yellowed with age, or containing old-style book cards.

8. Treat duplicate titles as separate works. This means that one might be retained and another weeded out.

9. Keep local authors, gift books, or special books of local subjects if you happen to recognize them. Do not worry about discarding valuable works, since the weeding manager will look at each book before it is discarded.

10. Do not make a subjective judgment about keeping a book because you think the author, subject, or title is important.

11. If you have any serious questions, ask the weeding supervisor.

12. Work as comfortably as possible. The use of different size stools will cut fatigue and increase productivity.

13. Your early selections will be double-checked by the weeding manager, who will give you any additional training you may need.

14. If for any reason you are interrupted in the middle of a shelf, turn the last book observed on its spine so that you can start from where you left off.

THE METHOD SUMMARIZED

The Book Card Method consists of taking a sample of 500 book cards at the circulation desk, representing the last 500 consecutive charge-outs. Then the most recent shelf-time periods are tabulated on the form shown on page 104, one entry for each book card. These shelf-time periods are described in terms of the year of previous use.

A percentage is computed for each year and cumulated, and a table results. See "Form: Summary,"* (page 104). A reasonable, arbitrary keeping level, say 96 percent, is established, and a cut-point is created. In the Warner Library, used as our example, all volumes used last in 1976 or earlier were weeded.

---

*The actual size of all forms used by the author was 8½x11 inches.

Form: Summary

9/12/80

Warner Library
Tarrytown, N.Y.

BOOK CARD METHOD

Form for Computing Cut Date
from Circulation Sample

Fiction only. One
week's circulation.

DATE	VOLUMES WITH THIS <u>PREVIOUS</u> DUE DATE	TOTAL #	%	CUM. %
1981				
1980	₩₩ ₩₩ ₩₩ ₩₩ ₩₩ ₩₩ ₩₩ ₩₩ ₩₩ ₩₩ ... (tally marks) ... ₩₩ ₩₩ ₩₩ ₩₩ ₩₩ |||	299	73.5	73.5%
1979	₩₩ ₩₩ ₩₩ ₩₩ ₩₩ ₩₩ ₩₩ ₩₩ ₩₩ ₩₩ ₩₩ ||||	59	14.5	88%
1978	₩₩ ₩₩ ₩₩ |	16	4	92%
1977	₩₩ ₩₩ ₩₩ ||	17	4	96%
1976	||||	4	1	97%
1975	||||	4	1	98%
1974	||	2	.5	98.5%
1973	₩₩	5	1	99.5%
1972	|	1	.5	100%
1971				
Pre 71				
	Total	407		

THE METHOD ILLUSTRATED

Step 1: Collect 500 book cards at the circulation station. It is important that this sample consist of book cards representing 500 consecutive circulations. Care must be taken to be sure that no book has been reslipped and returned to the shelf before its card was utilized in the sample. The safest procedure is to remove from the circulation station, each day, all the book cards collected.

Step 2: Tabulate all the required data and return the book cards to the circulation desk. The *second most recent year date* appearing on each book card is entered on "Form: Blank," below. Each book card generates only one entry, in

Form: Blank

BOOK CARD METHOD

Form for Computing Cut Date
from Circulation Sample

DATE	VOLUMES WITH THIS PREVIOUS DUE DATE	TOTAL #	TOTAL %	CUM. %
1981**				
1980				
1979				
1978				
1977				
1976				
1975				
1974				
1973				
1972				
1971				
Pre 71				
	Total			

**Note: The current year should appear in the top row and earlier years in each successive row.

the form of a small straight mark in the proper row, under the column entitled "VOLUMES WITH THIS PREVIOUS DATE DUE." The year to be entered is the *second most recent year* shown on the book card. All the book cards have had a future date stamped on them to indicate the date this book is due. Disregard this last date. Take the next most recent date. Here are a few examples:

DA Dixon, W.		E Fay, Paul Burgess	
687 Her Majesty's tower		842 The pleasure of his	
T7		F38 company	
D62			
DATE	**ISSUED TO**	**DATE**	**ISSUED TO**
SEP 3 0 1966		OCT 8 1977	
DEC 2 6 1972		JUN 4 1978	
AUG 4 1975		JUL 2 1 1978	
JUN 1 2 1978		DEC 3 1979	
JUN 3 0 1981		FEB 5 1980	
		AUG 1 1980	
		JUN 3 0 1981	

Q Yost, Edna	
130 Women of modern science	
Y63	
DATE	**ISSUED TO**
SEP 1 5 1979	
JUN 3 0 1981	

In the three examples given above, these cards were removed from the circulation desk on June 2, 1981, in a library having a four-week loan period. Note that each book card was stamped "Jun 30 1981," showing the current due date for a book now in circulation. This date is to be disregarded, as it measures the end of a shelf-time period, and the next most recent date, which indicates the beginning of that shelf-time period, is entered. The proper tabulation of these book cards is shown on the following "Form: Step 2."

Form: Step 2

BOOK CARD METHOD

Form for Computing Cut Date
from Circulation Sample

DATE	VOLUMES WITH THIS <u>PREVIOUS</u> DUE DATE	TOTAL #	TOTAL %	CUM. %
1981				
1980	ı			
1979	ı			
1978	ı			
1977				
1976				
1975				
1974				
1973				
1972				
1971				
Pre 71				
	Total			

Note that the first card generates a single mark entered in the line 1978, the second in 1980, and the third in 1979. Continue through the book cards entering all the usable data. In this example, from the Warner Library, the form now looks like "Form Step 2-A," page 108.

Form: Step 2-A

BOOK CARD METHOD

Form for Computing Cut Date
from Circulation Sample

DATE	VOLUMES WITH THIS PREVIOUS DUE DATE	TOTAL #	%	CUM. %
1981	[Study made in 1980]			
1980	ꞌꞀ ꞀꞀ ꞀꞀ ꞀꞀ (hand-tallied marks)			
1979	(hand-tallied marks) ꞀꞀ IIII			
1978	ꞀꞀ ꞀꞀ ꞀꞀ I			
1977	ꞀꞀ ꞀꞀ ꞀꞀ II			
1976	IIII			
1975	IIII			
1974	II			
1973	ꞀꞀ			
1972	I			
1971				
Pre 71				
	Total			

Step 3: Total the number of cases indicated for each year. Enter each result in the proper row under the column headed "TOTAL #." The form being filled in should now look like "Form: Step 3."

Form: Step 3

BOOK CARD METHOD

Form for Computing Cut Date
from Circulation Sample

DATE	VOLUMES WITH THIS <u>PREVIOUS</u> DUE DATE	TOTAL #	%	CUM. %
1981	[STUDY MADE IN 1980]			
1980	HHT HHT HHT HHT HHT HHT HHT HHT HHT HHT HHT HHT HHT HHT HHT HHT HHT HHT HHT HHT HHT HHT HHT HHT HHT HHT HHT HHT HHT HHT HHT HHT HHT HHT HHT HHT HHT HHT HHT HHT HHT HHT HHT HHT HHT HHT HHT HHT HHT HHT HHT HHT HHT HHT HHT HHT HHT HHT IIII	299		
1979	HHT HHT HHT HHT HHT HHT HHT HHT HHT HHT HHT IIII	59		
1978	HHT HHT HHT I	16		
1977	HHT HHT HHT II	17		
1976	IIII	4		
1975	IIII	4		
1974	II	2		
1973	HHT	5		
1972	I	1		
1971				
Pre 71				
	Total			

The system using a crossed line for every fifth case makes counting easier. The listing of exactly 50 cases in each row serves the same purpose.

In the above example, all the volumes whose last use was in 1980, as indicated in the cell headed "VOLUMES WITH THIS PREVIOUS DUE DATE," have been added together, and there were 299 cases of such use. The number 299 was entered in the proper column and row. Likewise, the 59 previus uses in 1979 were entered in the same column but the next row. This is continued until all of the samples that were recorded in accordance with their shelf-time periods (as expressed in terms of the date of their previous use) have been tallied.

Step 4: Add up the column that was just tabulated in Step 3. This column represents the total number of cases used in this sample. Enter this number on the bottom line alongside the word "Total." In this case, the number 407 was entered, and the form now looks like "Form: Step 4."

Form: Step 4

BOOK CARD METHOD

Form for Computing Cut Date
from Circulation Sample

DATE	VOLUMES WITH THIS PREVIOUS DUE DATE	TOTAL #	TOTAL %	CUM. %
1981	[STUDY MADE IN 1980]			
1980	₩₩ ₩₩ ₩₩ ₩₩ ₩₩ ₩₩ ₩₩ ₩₩ ₩₩ ₩₩ ₩₩ ₩₩ ₩₩ ₩₩ ₩₩ ₩₩ ₩₩ ₩₩ ₩₩ ₩₩ ₩₩ ₩₩ ₩₩ ₩₩ ₩₩ ₩₩ ₩₩ ₩₩ ₩₩ ₩₩ ₩₩ ₩₩ ₩₩ ₩₩ ₩₩ ₩₩ ₩₩ ₩₩ ₩₩ ₩₩ ₩₩ ₩₩ ₩₩ ₩₩ ₩₩ ₩₩ ₩₩ ₩₩ ₩₩ ₩₩ ₩₩ ₩₩ ₩₩ ₩₩ ₩₩ ₩₩ ₩₩ ₩₩ ₩₩ |||	299		
1979	₩₩ ₩₩ ₩₩ ₩₩ ₩₩ ₩₩ ₩₩ ₩₩ ₩₩ ₩₩ ₩₩ ||||	59		
1978	₩₩ ₩₩ ₩₩ |	16		
1977	₩₩ ₩₩ ₩₩ ||	17		
1976	||||	4		
1975	||||	4		
1974	||	2		
1973	₩₩	5		
1972	|	1		
1971				
Pre 71				
	Total	407		

Step 5: Compute the percentage of usage represented by each year. This percentage figure should be entered in the column directly to the right of the "TOTAL #" column, and is headed "TOTAL %." To compute the percentage for each year, divide the total number of uses in that year by the total number of cases in the entire sample. In "Form: Step 5," the 299 cases for 1980 were divided by the total number of cases in the sample, 407. This gave 73.5 percent, figured to the nearest half percent. Repeat the process for each successive year. In the Warner Library, this produced 14.5 percent for 1979; 4 percent for 1978; etc. Obviously, this computation can be made only for years in which some previous use was recorded on the form.

Form: Step 5

BOOK CARD METHOD

Form for Computing Cut Date
from Circulation Sample

DATE	VOLUMES WITH THIS <u>PREVIOUS</u> DUE DATE	TOTAL #	TOTAL %	CUM. %
1981	[STUDY MADE IN 1980]			
1980	(tally marks)	299	73.5	
1979	(tally marks)	59	14.5	
1978	(tally marks)	16	4	
1977	(tally marks)	17	4	
1976	IIII	4	1	
1975	IIII	4	1	
1974	II	2	.5	
1973	HHt	5	1	
1972	I	1	.5	
1971				
Pre 71				
	Total	407		

Step 6: Compute the cumulative percentage starting from the most recent year. Enter this figure in the column headed "CUM. %." *Cumulative percentage* results from the successive percentages being added together from the top to the bottom of the form. The form now looks like "Form: Step 6."

Form: Step 6

BOOK CARD METHOD

Form for Computing Cut Date
from Circulation Sample

DATE	VOLUMES WITH THIS <u>PREVIOUS</u> DUE DATE	TOTAL #	TOTAL %	CUM. %
1981	[STUDY MADE IN 1980]			
1980	(tally marks)	299	73.5	73.5%
1979	(tally marks)	59	14.5	88%
1978	⊞⊞ ⊞⊞ ⊞⊞ I	16	4	92%
1977	⊞⊞ ⊞⊞ ⊞⊞ II	17	4	96%
1976	IIII	4	1	97%
1975	IIII	4	1	98%
1974	II	2	.5	98.5%
1973	⊞⊞	5	1	99.5%
1972	I	1	.5	100%
1971				
Pre 71				
Total		407		

In our example, in the row designated "1980," 73.5 percent is carried over from the "TOTAL %" column and entered alongside in the "CUM. %" column. Going down one row, the 73.5 percent is added to the 14.5 percent, and 88 percent is written in the "1979" row. For the next year, 4 percent is added to the 88 percent, giving 92 percent, and so forth, until all the percentages have been added together. The total always should equal 100 percent. If, because of rounding, the resultant figure is not 100 percent, cumulate the total number of cases, year by year, and recompute the cumulative percentages. Thus, add the 299 cases to the 59 cases, and divide this new number (358) by the total number of cases (407). Enter this percentage in the cumulative % column. Now add the 16 cases in 1978 to the 358 (giving 374) and divide this number by 407. Continue this process until 100 percent of the cases have been cumulated and tabulated.

Step 7: Determine the keeping percentage to be used for weeding. This is an arbitrary decision to be made by the librarian, and is discussed at some length in Chapter 7. In general, for circulating collections, percentages from 95 to 98 percent have been used successfully by the author. This percentage is the statistically computed percentage of circulation that should be retained after weeding. The higher this percentage, the fewer the number of books that will be weeded. Therefore, it is recommended that the keeping level not exceed 96 percent unless special conditions dictate a higher keeping level. If there is any doubt as to what percentage to select, use 96 percent.

Step 8: Determine the cut-date to be used for weeding. Run your eye down the "CUM. %" column and draw a line *under* the box that contains the keeping percentage level just selected in Step 7. The form is now in its final condition. See "Form: Step 8," page 114. In the case of the Warner Library, the 96 percent level was chosen. (One of the reasons for this choice was that this selection included an entire year as the cut-date.) Now read in the left-hand column the years divided by the line just drawn. This is interpreted as follows: Keep all volumes used last in 1977 or more recently; weed all volumes used last in 1976 or before. The cut-point has now been determined. It is December 31, 1976.

A few special conditions might exist which relate to the determination of the cut-date. If the keeping percentage creates a line that does not include an entire year, two possible solutions are suggested. For example, on "Form: Step 8," suppose one wanted to retain 95 percent of the predicted future usage. This would produce a line running somewhere inside the box marked 1977. The box 1978 shows 92 percent and the box 1977 shows 96 percent. What does one do?

A. The simplest method is to estimate a month which would divide the box proportionately to the percentage required. In this case, 95 percent is three-quarters of the way between 92 and 96 percent. Therefore, if a cut-date of March 31, 1977 were used, it is likely that the weeder would retain 95 percent of the future usage of the collection. In this case, the month as well as the year would have to be used as the cut-point. Here all volumes used in the last nine months (three-fourths) of 1977 are retained in the core collection. Volumes used last since March 31, 1977 would be retained; those used last in January, February, or March 1977 and earlier would be weeded.

B. A more precise way to compute the date to be used as a cut-point, in the above example, is to pull out all the book cards indicating

Form: Step 8

BOOK CARD METHOD

Form for Computing Cut Date
from Circulation Sample

DATE	VOLUMES WITH THIS <u>PREVIOUS</u> DUE DATE	TOTAL #	%	CUM. %
1981	[STUDY MADE IN 1980]			
1980	ᚆᚆ ᚆᚆ ᚆᚆ ᚆᚆ ᚆᚆ ᚆᚆ ᚆᚆ ᚆᚆ ᚆᚆ ᚆᚆ (tally marks)	299	73.5	73.5%
1979	ᚆᚆ ᚆᚆ ᚆᚆ ᚆᚆ ᚆᚆ ᚆᚆ ᚆᚆ ᚆᚆ ᚆᚆ ᚆᚆ ᚆᚆ IIII	59	14.5	88%
1978	ᚆᚆ ᚆᚆ ᚆᚆ I	16	4	92%
1977	ᚆᚆ ᚆᚆ ᚆᚆ II	17	4	96%
1976	IIII	4	1	97%
1975	IIII	4	1	98%
1974	II	2	.5	98.5%
1973	ᚆᚆ	5	1	99.5%
1972	I	1	.5	100%
1971				
Pre 71				
	Total	407		

the most recent previous usage in 1977. You will have 17 cards in
hand. Put them in chronological order. List these previous dates
in reverse chronological order, as follows:

DATE	CUM. # of Samples	CUM. %	CUT-POINTS
December 16, 1977	375	92.0%	
November 9, 1977	376	92.0%	
October 28, 1977 October 26, 1977	378	93.0%	93%
September 13, 1977 September 9, 1977 September 5, 197	381	93.5%	
August 17, 1977	382	94.0%	94%
July 11, 1977	383	94.5%	
June 10, 1977	384	94.5%	
May 23, 1977	385	94.5%	
April 1, 1977	386	95.0%	95% ◄—
➤ March 11, 1977	387	95.0%	
February 15, 1977 February 9, 1977	389	95.5%	
January 21, 1977 January 7, 1977	391	96.0%	96%

Now select the fifth oldest date, the number selected being approximately one-fourth of 17 plus 1. This date becomes the keeping-point, and the month, day, and year may be used for this purpose. In the above list, an arrow in the left-hand column points to the designated date. This gives a keeping-point of March 11, 1977. All books used on that date or more recently would be retained. The cut-point is March 10, 1977.

C. A third method of computation can be undertaken by tabulating the cumulative total number of samples for each month, and dividing this number by the total number of cases (407) in the entire sample. The above table shows this in columns 2 and 3. Here 386 was divided by 407 giving the result of 95 percent. Now the keeping-point becomes April 1 and the cut-point March 31, 1977. An arrow in the right-hand column points to the designated percentage.

It can be seen that these three methods have produced slightly different results. Such differences are insignificant, and therefore the simplest method is preferred. From a point of view of convenience, it is advisable, wherever possible, to select a keeping percentage which encompasses an entire year.

Step 9: In the circulating collection, examine the book card of every book on the shelves and remove all volumes not having dates more recent than the cut-point date. This is the actual weeding process. One book at a time is removed from the shelf, and the book card is examined carefully. In the Warner Library, if *the most recent date* appearing on a book card were 1977 or more recent, the book was replaced on the shelf; if it were 1976 or earlier, the book was removed from the shelf and was considered a candidate for weeding. It is not necessary to inspect the cards of books in circulation since they *all* have recent dates stamped on their cards.

This is not a professional job. The work of removing the volumes from the shelves can be done by non-librarians — either clerks or volunteer workers.

Step 10: Inspect all candidates for weeding and return to the shelves those volumes not to be weeded out. This is a professional job and should be done by the head librarian, the acquisitions librarian, or whomever is responsible for building the library collection and maintaining its integrity. Here, judgment is involved. It is axiomatic that the fewer books returned to the shelves the better the collection will be.

THE PROBLEM OF BOOK CARDS WITH NO DUE DATE INDICATED

The most serious practical weeding problem relates to the book whose book card has no due date stamped on it. This might involve from 10 to over 50 percent of the book cards. They should be treated as follows:

1. Newly acquired books may not have been given an adequate opportunity to circulate. They should not be weeded if they have been acquired more recently than the cut-point date. Accession numbers frequently give enough information so that this decision can be made intelligently. Otherwise, a reasonable guess, based upon imprint date, for example, might be in order. If in doubt, do not weed it out, but mark the current date on the book card to prevent a recurrence of the problem on the next weeding.

2. A more serious problem relates to older books with new book cards, usually supplied after rebinding or because the old book card was used up or damaged. Again, some guesswork may be used to judge whether or not the new card was created before or after the cut-point date. If in doubt, do not weed these volumes out, but date the book cards.

3. Older books with older book cards containing no due dates are easier to handle. This situation normally means that no use was made of the volume since the cut-date. These books should be considered candidates for weeding. If a real doubt exists, date the book card with the current date and leave it for the next weeding.

SUBSTITUTE BOOK CARD METHOD

Certain charging machines apply a small colored dot to the back of the book card when a book is being charged out. If this colored dot has been color-coded so that the year of its application can be decoded, and if the year is missing from the due-date stamp on the book card, the colored dot can be used to create the weeding cut-point.

Certain extra steps are required for this technique to be of use. The year that any specific color was used must be identified. This often can be done by noting the copyright year of relatively new volumes and noting the successive colors applied to the book card.

Additional Steps:

Step 1: Identify the year during which a specific colored dot was being used. A written list should be created showing the results achieved, as follows:

Color Decoding List

Dot Color	Year Represented
Red	1973
Green	1974
Blue	1975
Black	1976
Purple	1977
Yellow	1978
Orange	1979
Pink	1980
Gray	1981

Step 2: Follow weeding steps 1 through 10, just described, using the colored dot as the source of the year of previous circulation. This step makes the entire process more arduous since one must find the most recently applied colored dot on each book card, or the one previous to that. It requires that one refer constantly to the decoding list in order to interpret properly the colored dots. If the colored dots are not in some kind of predetermined order chronologically, this method becomes rather cumbersome.

A Special Case

If the due-date stamp color has been changed yearly but no year was stamped on the book card, use the above method substituting the colored due-date stamp for the colored dot.

THE SIMPLIFIED BOOK CARD METHOD OF WEEDING

The Simplified Book Card Method of weeding is recommended to weeders who feel comfortable with mathematical computation. It involves one basic change in the normal Book Card Method of weeding described earlier in this chapter. It replaces tabulating steps 2, 3, 4, 5, and 6 with a mechanical operation. This is the major modification of the regular method.

The Method Summarized

The method uncovers the cut-point *without* the use of the form (Form: Blank, p. 105) recommended in the earlier method. Instead, it arranges the book cards in chronological order, using the previous due date for this purpose, and selects the one card containing the relevant cut-date. For instance, if the collection were to be weeded at the 96 percent keeping level, the proper card is located as follows: If there were 400 cards in the sample, the card containing the 384th oldest previous due date would produce the 96 percent keeping-date (multiply 400 by 96 percent). The 385th card contains the cut-date.

The Method Illustrated

Step 1: Collect 500 book cards at the circulation station as described in Step 1, p. 105.

Step 2: Determine the keeping percentage to be used for weeding, as in Step 7, p. 113. For purposes of this example, 96 percent will be used.

Step 3: Convert the keeping percentage into the weeding loss percentage. This is done by subtracting the keeping percentage from 100 percent. In the example, 100 percent minus 96 percent equal 4 percent.

Step 4: Multiply the number of cards in the sample by the weeding loss percentage selected. In the example used earlier in this chapter (Form: Summary, p. 119), there were 407 useful samples. Multiply this number by 4 percent and round to the nearest whole number. This gives 16.

Step 5: Sort the book cards into piles by year of previous use (as above), in reverse chronological order: the most current year first, the second most recent year next, etc. In the example used, there would be 299 cards in the first pile representing 1980, 59 for 1979 in the second, 16 for 1978 in the third, etc. (See Form: Summary).

Step 6: Select the pile containing the card showing the cut-date. In the example, the card containing the sixteenth oldest previous due date should be located. That card is in the pile representing the 1976 uses.

Step 7: Take this pile of cards and put them in reverse chronological order by year of previous use. In the example, those four cards contained the following dates and were put in this order:

> Dec 11, 1976
> Sept 4, 1976
> June 12, 1976
> Jan 23, 1976

Step 8: Select the card containing the cut-date. There were 12 cards with dates older than 1976. Jan 23, 1976 was the thirteenth oldest, June 12, 1976 the fourteenth, etc.

Dates Found	Chronological # from Oldest
Dec 11, 1976	16th
Sept 4, 1976	15th
June 12, 1976	14th
Jan 23, 1976	13th

The cut-date becomes Dec 11, 1976.

Form: Summary

9/12/80

Warner Library
Tarrytown, N.Y.

BOOK CARD METHOD

Form for Computing Cut Date
from Circulation Sample

Fiction only. One
week's circulation.

DATE	VOLUMES WITH THIS <u>PREVIOUS</u> DUE DATE	TOTAL #	%	CUM. %
1981				
1980	‖‖‖ ‖‖‖ ‖‖‖ ‖‖‖ ‖‖‖ ‖‖‖ ‖‖‖ ‖‖‖ ‖‖‖ ‖‖‖ (many tally marks) ‖‖\	299	73.5	73.5%
1979	‖‖‖ IIII	59	14.5	88%
1978	‖‖‖ ‖‖‖ ‖‖‖ I	16	4	92%
1977	‖‖‖ ‖‖‖ ‖‖‖ II	17	4	96%
1976	IIII	4	1	97%
1975	IIII	4	1	98%
1974	II	2	.5	98.5%
1973	‖‖‖	5	1	99.5%
1972	I	1	.5	100%
1971				
Pre 71				
	Total	407		

Step 9: Weed the collection keeping any volume used since the cut-date, and removing all volumes used last on the cut-date or before. In the example, keep all volumes used Dec 12, 1976 or more recently, and weed those last used Dec 11, 1976 or earlier.

Step 10: Inspect all candidates for weeding and return to the shelves those volumes not to be weeded out, as in Step 10, p. 116.

METHODS TO IMPROVE FUTURE WEEDING

Present procedures in the library frequently make the use of the Book Card Method of weeding less reliable than it could be. It is suggested that all libraries using the book card method of circulation control augment the present procedures with the following:

1. All new books should have an initial date stamped on the book card when the book is being processed. Ideally this should be the date the book is shelved. This gives a starting date to assist in measuring the shelf-time period, and prevents the weeding of a newer book which hasn't had a chance to circulate.

2. Whenever books are rebound and new book cards are inserted, the date of last use should be brought forward from the old card to the new one.

3. Whenever a book card is replaced because there is no more room on it for new due dates (or for any other reason), the date of last use should be carried forward as the first entry on the new card.

4. When books are returned to the library after being long overdue, the date of reshelving ought to be entered on the book card. This prevents a book which had no chance to circulate from being weeded prematurely.

5. When books have been held in the librarian's office or taken out of normal use by the staff, the date of shelving the book in publicly accessible places should be added to the book card.

6. Reserved volumes and non-circulating volumes, such as reference or ready-reference works, should be shelved by the library staff after being used, and the book card should be dated to indicate such usage.

7. Due dates should be stamped on book cards in chronological order instead of in random order so that the most recent activity can be identified easily.

SOME THEORY: CURRENT CIRCULATION PATTERNS
VS. LONG-RANGE CIRCULATION PATTERNS

The Book Card Method of weeding has been based, in part, upon an assumption some people find difficult to accept: that the patterns of circulation do not change significantly over a long period of time. It further assumes that a sample of the circulation taken for a week, more or less, has the same shelf-time period characteristics as a sample taken over 5 or even 10 years. It assumes that such shelf-time characteristics will remain unchanged in the future.

All of these assumptions have been tested carefully, and there is strong evidence that they are valid. They have been reported upon elsewhere in this volume. A new study was made in Larchmont to test the long- and short-term shelf-time characteristics. Table 7 shows the result of this study.

Table 7
CURRENT SHELF-TIME PERIODS VS. LONG-TERM SHELF-TIME PERIODS

Shelf-Time Period Under	Cumulative % of Use Having This Shelf-Time Period	
	Source: *1 week's current* *circulation*	*Source:* *Last 10 years of* *circulation*
2 years	96%	95%
3 years	98%	97%
4 years	99%	99%
5 years	99%	99%
6 years	99%	99%
7 years	99%	100%
8 years	100%	
9 years	100%	
10 years	100%	

The differences in percentages reflected in the chart are statistically insignificant. It can be assumed that a sample of circulation in the Larchmont Library, taken over a current one-week period, has the same shelf-time period characteristics as a sample taken over 10 years.

11

WHEN TO USE IT

The Spine-Marking Method should be used only when other methods cannot be used, for it involves a substantial time lag before weeding can be undertaken. It is the method of last resort. The other methods use information already created and recorded. The Spine-Marking Method starts to create the needed data only on the day it is put into effect. In this respect, it must continue to be applied until a *weeding signal* is received—a period of time that could extend from a minimum of 1 year to a practical maximum of 5 or even 10 years. This method should be used only where no history of book use has been recorded.

ADVANTAGES OF THE METHOD

This method is applicable to some of the volumes in *every* library. In every library, no matter what systems are in effect, part of the usage tends to go unrecorded, or if recorded, such records are not usable for weeding purposes. At the least, the unrecorded usage normally includes the in-library usage by both the clients and the staff.

There are a number of other advantages to the method:

1. **The Spine-Marking Method can be used to assist in weeding at any time,** even before a weeding signal is received. This is due to the fact that a spine-marked volume is automatically a member of the core collection and should never be considered for weeding. This reduces the number of volumes which have to be considered as likely weeding candidates, even if subjective weeding criteria are to be applied.

2. **The actual weeding itself can be done more rapidly than by any other method known.** While the wait for the ultimate weeding signal may be long, once it is received things move very rapidly. One merely removes all volumes lacking a spine mark.

3. **The weeding itself is a low-cost operation.** This work can be done by untrained volunteers or any other form of low cost labor—a considerable asset in these times of financial belt-tightening.

4. **The spine mark can be a potent tool to assist in the acquisition of books.** As the spine-marking process proceeds, it becomes apparent that in some segments of the collection many volumes are spine-marked and in other segments very few volumes are. By focusing acquisition efforts in the most heavily marked areas, substantial usage for new acquisitions is assured, and as far as client satisfaction is concerned, the library optimizes the money it has spent for books. The spine-marking technique can become a major tool for creating a library where the classes of volumes held are numerically proportionate to the relative use of those classes.

5. **Spine-marking permits an ongoing weeding procedure** which can be built in to the normal, long-term routines of the library, and with relatively little thought or effort, weeding can be done on a continuing basis. By changing the color of the dots used for spine-marking (dotting over old dots is suggested), one can start setting up a new shelf-time period as soon as the previous weeding operation has been completed. Since books move constantly from the core to the non-core collection, this continuous weeding will keep the collection vital and fresh.

6. **The spine-marking procedure is simple, and of the methods recommended it involves the least amount of mathematical computation or manipulation of the data.**

STEPS TO BE TAKEN BEFORE WEEDING

Step 1: Appoint a weeding manager. This operation may take from one to perhaps five or more years, so the manager should be a senior staff member likely to be around for that period of time.

Step 2: Organize the entire operation. A complete plan should be created, in writing, covering the following points.

A. Establish the date on which the weeding procedure shall be started.

B. Establish reporting forms to assure that all people involved are cooperating. Reports on numbers of books dotted each day might help encourage such cooperation. Those involved are all the people who: charge out volumes; process books; reshelve books; and all library personnel using books in the library. Practically all people working for the library are involved in one way or another.

C. Schedule and hold training sessions with each group of workers, defining their tasks as follows:

Clerks at circulation stations: Spine-mark all undotted books as they are charged out. Tabulate the number of books dotted and undotted monthly, or as scheduled.

Clerks discharging books: Spine-mark all books which are undotted and are being returned after circulating.

Shelving clerks: Before reshelving, spine-mark all undotted volumes. These are the books which have just been discharged or have experienced in-library use.

Personnel processing new acquisitions: All new books are to be spine-marked before being shelved for the first time.

All other personnel: Spine-mark all volumes you have used and are reshelving. Reference librarians must tabulate monthly the data relating to volumes dotted or undotted in order to recognize the weeding signal.

D. **Procure all supplies and forms needed.** These include enough Avery self-adhering dots to spine-mark every book in the library twice. One-quarter inch dots, all of one color, have been used successfully. Also, produce 50 to 100 sets of the two forms shown on pages 202 and 203.

E. **Supply dots to all library personnel using them.**

F. **Notify the library's patrons as to what is happening and instruct them not to reshelve volumes used in the library.** Signs and publicity help, but the library staff must be prepared to supervise and enforce this new rule.

G. **Organize the weeding operation when the weeding signal is received.** Follow the suggestions listed in Step 2, for the Book Card Method of weeding (pp. 101, 102).

Step 3: Pre-test the various procedures recommended in the step-by-step descriptions. The weeding manager should perform each operation personally, until familiar and comfortable with each step. Make sure no major hitches arise, that all kinks and doubts have been worked out, and that each step is understood.

TRAINING THE PERSONNEL INVOLVED

In order to assist in the training of personnel, the following instructions should be included in the recommended training sessions:

Instructions for Weeding

1. For every volume used, apply two small dots to the book's spine, one inch from the bottom edge of the book. (This location should be changed if necessary so that call numbers are not obscured.) If the book has been dotted previously, do not add dots. For all circulating books, the dotting should take place: at the charge-out station, at the discharge station, and when the book is being reshelved. This triple procedure is used to make sure that the book does not slip through unmarked.

2. All volumes added to the collection should be spine-marked before they are shelved. This prevents new additions from being weeded before being given an opportunity to be used.

3. For books which have experienced in-library use:

   a. Clients should not reshelve them. Clerks should spine-mark them before placing them back on the shelves.

   b. Reference works used only by the staff (such as ready-reference works) should be spine-marked by the user before they are returned to the shelves.

4. If volumes are rebound, the spine-marking indication should be carried forward to the new binding. If such volumes have no spine mark on them, they should be left unmarked. (It is very likely that books not spine-marked should not be rebound.)

5. A program should be undertaken to make sure that clients do not remove the spine mark. Explain what is going on, what the dots mean, and their importance. Watch out for young children who might think that these dots were put on the books for their personal pleasure, and who like to remove such dots.

6. Make sure that all volumes used are spine-marked. Carelessness in this activity will result in weeding out the very books that should be retained. Supervisors should check daily to make sure that the work is being done. When the routine is firmly established, monthly checks should still be made.

7. Overdue books, books kept out for very long periods of time (say all summer), books kept in staff offices, and other books not permitted to circulate normally should be spine-marked before shelving as if they were new acquisitions.

THE METHOD SUMMARIZED

The Spine-Marking Method measures and records the shelf-time period characteristics of that part of the collection being used. It involves applying two self-adhesive dots to the spine of each volume used. The spine mark establishes the beginning of a shelf-time period, which is then used to determine when weeding should occur.

If, for instance, after applying these dots for one year every subsequent volume used by library clients had been previously dotted, there would have been created a shelf-time period of one year, which would represent 100 percent of current usage. All of the volumes enjoying current use must have been dotted previously sometime during the last year, since that is when the dotting was being done. If one now removed all undotted volumes from the shelves, *100 percent* of all future usage will be retained by the remaining core collection.

In actual practice, the 100 percent keeping level is too high to result in substantial weeding. Therefore, as discussed elsewhere, some lower level is selected. Thus, for example, when 96 percent (or whatever other level has been predetermined) of the volumes being used have been previously dotted, the weeding signal has been received and all undotted volumes on the shelves are weeded.

THE METHOD ILLUSTRATED

This method involves several separate but sometimes overlapping approaches:

I. The procedure applied to books circulating:

   A. When weeding the library as one entity.
   B. When weeding by class.

II. The procedure applied to books in the circulating collection which experience in-library use.

III. The procedure applied to books which do not circulate, used by clients (and perhaps by the staff) in the library.

IV. The procedure applied to books which do not circulate, used by the staff in the library and which are reshelved by the staff.

Each of these procedures is somewhat different from the other. However, wherever the same subset of the collection is being used in different ways, the relevant weeding procedures must be applied simultaneously. For example, procedures I and II above both involve the circulating collection and should be undertaken at the same time. On the other hand, the ready-reference collection, used only be reference librarians, may be weeded independently of the rest of the collection at any time.

The Procedure for Weeding Books Circulating
When Weeding the Library as an Entity

Step 1: Apply two dots to the spine of every volume as it circulates. Only one set of dots is required on each volume so that the dotting process becomes one of decreasing effort as time passes. For instance, on the first day all volumes circulating must be dotted. A few months later perhaps only half have to be dotted, since the rest were previously dotted. At one year, perhaps 90 percent are already dotted, so only the remaining 10 percent must be dotted. And just before the 96 percent weeding signal is received, only 4 percent of the volumes need be dotted.

The two dots are placed in a standardized, predetermined position, such as "centered on the spine, one-half inch from the bottom edge," as shown below:

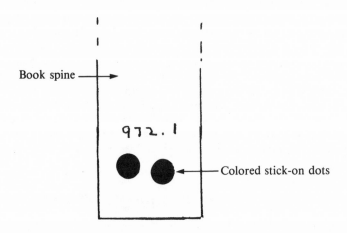

Make sure that the dots do not obscure the classification number. Two dots are used to improve the reliability and security of the system, to prevent the loss of information in case one of the dots should fall off or be removed.

The handling of dots has proved awkward at times. It has been suggested that a book-marking labeling gun might simplify the spine-marking procedure.

Step 2: If not already dotted, apply two dots to the spine of every volume as it comes back from the client. This step has two purposes. In the early stages of the procedure, it dots volumes which were out and are undotted because the Spine-Marking Method had not yet begun. This speeds up the process somewhat. Secondly, and more importantly, it is a double check: to make sure that the books did not pass through the charge-out station without being dotted, or that dots have not fallen off or been removed. If Step 1 has been applied rigorously, this second step will involve very few volumes after the first month.

Step 3: If not already dotted, apply two dots to the spine of every volume being reshelved. This is a triple check, since the volumes have been processed previously upon being charged and discharged. This step is essential if the core collection is to be identified properly. It is important that core collection volumes are not weeded out because of careless spine-marking.

Step 4: One year after the dotting has been started, and monthly thereafter, tabulate whether the books being charged out have been previously dotted or not. Use "Form: Step 4."

Form: Step 4

SPINE-MARKING METHOD

Date

Form for Recording Whether Books are Dotted or

Undotted at Circulation Station

Class	Dotted	Total	Undotted	Total

This is the basic data taken to establish the cut-point used for weeding. It is essential that this be done carefully and regularly. The tabulation should be made at all stations charging out books, and should be done simultaneously at all stations. The data indicates whether or not a volume had been dotted prior to this circulation. The one-year waiting period is used to prevent seasonal books from being weeded prematurely.

At this stage enter 100 consecutive circulations. After the tabulation, the form could look something like "Form: Step 4A."

Form: Step 4A

SPINE-MARKING METHOD

Form for Recording Whether Books are Dotted or _DATE 3/1/81_

Undotted at Circulation Station

Class	Dotted	Total	Undotted	Total
Entire Collection	HH HHT HHT HHT HHT HHT HHT HHT HHT HHT HHT HHT HHT HHT HHT III		HHT HHT HHT HHT HHT II	

Step 5: Add up the number of samples identified as "dotted" and "undotted," and enter the totals in the relevant columns. Here 73 books had been previously dotted; 27 had not. See "Form: Step 5."

Form: Step 5

SPINE-MARKING METHOD

Form for Recording Whether Books are Dotted or *DATE* **3/1/81**

Undotted at Circulation Station

Class	Dotted	Total	Undotted	Total
Entire Collection	HIT HIT HIT HIT HIT HIT HIT HIT HIT HIT HIT HIT HIT HIT III	73	HIT HIT HIT HIT HIT II	27

Step 6: Enter these totals on the new form, "Form: Step 6," as shown on page 130.

Form: Step 6

SPINE-MARKING METHOD

DATE 3/1/81

Form for Recognizing Weeding Signal:
Summary of Current Circulation Patterns

Classification	Total Book Circulation	Total No. Dotted	Total No. Undotted	% Dotted
Entire Collection		73	27	
TOTAL				

Step 7: Add these two totals together and enter on the form in the column headed "Total Book Circulation." The result (100) is shown on "Form: Step 7."

Form: Step 7

SPINE-MARKING METHOD

DATE 3/1/81

Form for Recognizing Weeding Signal:

Summary of Current Circulation Patterns

Classification	Total Book Circulation	Total No. Dotted	Total No. Undotted	% Dotted
Entire Collection	100	73	27	
TOTAL				

Step 8: Compute the percentage of volumes dotted and enter in the column headed "% Dotted." The computation is made by dividing the "Total No. Dotted" (73) by the "Total Book Circulation" (100). In this case, the result is 73 percent. The completed form should look like "Form: Step 8," on page 132.

Step 9: Determine the keeping percentage to be used for weeding. This is an arbitrary decision to be made by the librarian, and is discussed at some length in Chapter 7. In general, for circulating collections, percentages from 95 to 98 percent have been used successfully by the author. This percentage is the statistically computed percentage of circulation that should be retained after weeding. The higher this percentage, the fewer the number of books that will be weeded. Therefore, it is recommended that the keeping level not exceed 96 percent unless special conditions dictate a higher keeping level. If there is any doubt as to what percentage to select, use 96 percent.

Form: Step 8

SPINE-MARKING METHOD

Form for Recognizing Weeding Signal:
Summary of Current Circulation Patterns

DATE 3/1/81

Classification	Total Book Circulation	Total No. Dotted	Total No. Undotted	% Dotted
Entire Collection	100	73	27	73%
TOTAL				

Step 10: Continue to tabulate the data created by 100 consecutive circulations, once each month. During this tabulation period, continue the regular dotting procedures. These are not suspended until the weeding has been completed. When the 96 percent level is reached, go to Step 11.

Step 11: When the 96 percent keeping level (or whatever other level was determined in Step 9) is reached, tabulate the data from the next 400 consecutive circulations. When the weeding signal is received, your two forms should look like "Form: Step 11A" and "Form: Step 11B," page 134. If 400 cases do not produce the 96 percent or higher figure, wait one month and tabulate 400 cases again. Repeat this tabulating until the 96 percent keeping level is reached.

Step 12: Go through the entire circulating collection and remove all undotted volumes from the shelves. This is the actual weeding process. You have removed the non-core volumes, all of which are candidates for weeding. The volumes remaining on the shelves after weeding will retain 96 percent or more of the current circulation. The volumes currently in circulation need not be checked or examined, since all of them have been dotted.

This work can be done by non-librarians, either clerks or volunteer workers, and can be done very rapidly.

Form: Step 11A

SPINE-MARKING METHOD

DATE 11/1/81

Form for Recording Whether Books are Dotted or

Undotted at Circulation Station

Class	Dotted	Total	Undotted	Total
Entire Collection	LHT LHT HHT LHT LHT HHT HHT LHT LHT LHT HHT LHT LHT LHT LHT HHT LHT LHT LHT LHT HHT HHT LHT LHT HHT LHT HHT LHT LHT LHT LHT HHT LHT LHT LHT HHT HHT HHT LHT LHT HHT HHT LHT LHT HHT HHT HHT LHT LHT HHT HHT HHT LHT HHT HHT LHT HHT HHT LHT LHT HHT LHT LHT LHT LHT LHT HHT LHT LHT LHT LHT HHT LHT HHT LHT HHT IIII	384	LHT LHT HHT I	16

Step 13: Inspect all candidates for weeding and return to the shelves those volumes not to be weeded out. This is a professional job and should be done by the head librarian, the acquisitions librarian, or whomever is responsible for building the library collection and maintaining its integrity. Here, judgment is involved. It is axiomatic that the fewer books returned to the shelves the better the collection will be.

Form: Step 11B

SPINE-MARKING METHOD

Form for Recognizing Weeding Signal: *DATE 11/1/81*

Summary of Current Circulation Patterns

Classification	Total Book Circulation	Total No. Dotted	Total No. Undotted	% Dotted
Entire Collection	400	384	16	96%
TOTAL				

The Procedure for Books Circulating
When Weeding the Library by Class

The identical procedures, Steps 1 through 13 above, are followed, with the following modifications:

Modification 1: The form for identifying whether books are dotted or undotted is modified to identify the classes to be weeded. See "Form: M-1."

Form: M-1

SPINE-MARKING METHOD

D ATE

Form for Recording Whether Books are Dotted or

Undotted at Circulation Station

Class	Dotted	Total	Undotted	Total
FICTION				
MYSTERIES				
SCIENCE FICTION				
PAPER BACKS				
000-99				
100-199				
200-299				
300-399				
400-499				
500-599				
600-699				
700-799				
800-899				
900-999				
BIOGS				

This example relates to a library using the Dewey Classification notation with certain arbitrary classes added: biographies, mysteries, science fiction, paperbacks. Any kind of logical classification is workable. Some that have been used in the field include: fiction and non-fiction; adult and children's collections; and classes by type of material — books, records, magazines, tapes, etc.

Modification 2: Instead of 100 samples being recorded monthly, an attempt should be made to tabulate 100 samples for each class. However, if an early strong indication exists to show that more time is needed to reach 96 percent, fewer samples are acceptable. "Form: M-2A" and "Form: M-2B," pages 136 and 137, show actual data signalling that 96 percent is some months off, and further data collection can be put off for another month. The one exception is in class 400-499, where further tabulation should be continued at this time.

Form: M-2A

SPINE-MARKING METHOD   *HARRISON P.L.*

Form for Recording Whether Books are Dotted or

Undotted at Circulation Station

Class	Dotted	Total	Undotted	Total
FICTION	~~HHt~~ ~~HHt~~ ~~HHt~~ ~~HHt~~ ~~HHt~~ ~~HHt~~ ~~HHt~~ ~~HHt~~ ~~HHt~~ ~~HHt~~ INADEQUATE SPACE SEE M-2C (see p. 138, containing all information belonging here.)	240	~~HHt~~ ~~HHt~~	37
MYSTERIES				
SCIENCE FICTION				
PAPER BACKS	~~HHt~~ ~~HHt~~ ~~HHt~~ ~~HHt~~ ~~HHt~~ ~~HHt~~ II	32	~~HHt~~ ~~HHt~~ II	12
000–99	~~HHt~~ I	6	I	1
100–199	~~HHt~~ ~~HHt~~	10	IIII	4
200–299	II	2	I	1
300–399	~~HHt~~ ~~HHt~~ ~~HHt~~ ~~HHt~~ ~~HHt~~ ~~HHt~~ ~~HHt~~ ~~HHt~~ ~~HHt~~	45	~~HHt~~ ~~HHt~~ ~~HHt~~ ~~HHt~~ I	21
400–499	III	3		0
500–599	~~HHt~~ ~~HHt~~ I	11	~~HHt~~ III	8
600–699	~~HHt~~ ~~HHt~~ ~~HHt~~ ~~HHt~~ ~~HHt~~ IIII	29	~~HHt~~ ~~HHt~~ III	13
700–799	~~HHt~~ ~~HHt~~ ~~HHt~~ ~~HHt~~ ~~HHt~~ ~~HHt~~	30	~~HHt~~ ~~HHt~~ ~~HHt~~ II	17
800–899	~~HHt~~ ~~HHt~~ ~~HHt~~ II	17	~~HHt~~ ~~HHt~~ ~~HHt~~ I	16
900–999	~~HHt~~ ~~HHt~~ ~~HHt~~ ~~HHt~~ II	22	~~HHt~~ ~~HHt~~ ~~HHt~~ IIII	19
BIOGS	~~HHt~~ ~~HHt~~ II	12	IIII	4

Form: M-2B

SPINE-MARKING METHOD

Form for Recognizing Weeding Signal:
Summary of Current Circulation Patterns

*HARRISON
PUBLIC
LIBRARY*

Classification	Total Book Circulation	Total No. Dotted	Total No. Undotted	% Dotted
FICTION	277	240	37	89%
MYSTERIES				
SCIENCE FICTION				
PAPER BACKS	44	32	12	73
000–099	7	6	1	86
100–199	14	10	4	71
200–299	3	2	1	67
300–399	66	45	21	68
400–499	3	3	0	100
500–599	19	11	8	58
600–699	42	29	13	69
700–799	47	30	17	64
800–899	33	17	16	52
900–999	41	22	19	54
BIOGS	16	12	4	75
TOTAL	612	459	153	75%

Also note that even though these original forms actually measured 8½x11 inches, the amount of space available for tabulating fiction is too small. Use a supplemental form when that situation occurs. See "Form: M-2C."

Form: M-2C

SPINE-MARKING METHOD

HARRISON PUBLIC LIBRARY

Form for Recording Whether Books are Dotted or
Undotted at Circulation Station
Supplemental Work Sheet

Class	Dotted	Total	Undotted	Total
FICTION ONLY (see FORMS: m-2A & m-2B)	```(tally marks)```	240	```(tally marks)```	37

Modification 3: Continue the spine-marking procedure until all classes to be weeded have been weeded. When weeding the library as one entity, the first spine-marking process stops when the library is weeded. If spine-marking is continued in order to establish a new shelf-time period for the next weeding, the color of the dots is changed. In weeding by class, continue dotting with the same color until the last class is weeded. Since after weeding a class all volumes of that class are already dotted, the dotting task becomes progressively easier to perform.

Modification 4: When the weeding signal is received for any class, be sure to weed only that class. "Form: M-2D" shows an actual result where three classes are ready to be weeded at the 95 percent level, although 400 samples should be obtained for each of these three classes.

Form: M-2D

SPINE-MARKING METHOD

Form for Recognizing Weeding Signal:
Summary of Current Circulation Patterns

HARRISON PUBLIC LIBRARY

Classification	Total Book Circulation	Total No. Dotted	Total No. Undotted	% Dotted	
FICTION	272	259	13	95%	←
PAPER BACKS	29	26	3	90%	
BIOGS	16	14	2	88%	
000–99	3	2	1	67%	
100–199	9	9	0	100%	←
200–299	4	3	1	75%	
300–399	42	34	8	81%	
400–499	3	1	2	33%	
500–599	14	12	2	86%	
600–699	39	37	2	95%	←
700–799	58	46	12	79%	
800–899	20	16	4	80%	
900–999	72	59	13	82%	
SUBTOTAL 000–999	309	259	50	84%	
TOTAL	581	518	63	89%	

The Weeding Procedure for Books in the Circulating Collection Which Experience In-Library Use

This procedure should be undertaken simultaneously with the procedure recommended for books circulating.

Modification 1: The basic modification is that **clients must be instructed not to reshelve works used in the library, but to leave them either on the work tables**

or in special holding areas. **The clerks reshelving these works must be sure to double-dot all unmarked volumes being reshelved.** Then, Steps 3 through 13 for weeding circulating books (pp. 127-133) should be followed.

The Procedure for Weeding Books Which Do Not Circulate, but Are Used by Clients in the Library

The weeding of non-circulating collections is an operation independent of the weeding of circulating collections. It can be done at any time, and involves most of the procedures used for circulating volumes.

Step 1: Inform clients not to reshelve works used in the library. This regulation must be enforced, and volumes should be returned to designated holding areas.

Step 2: Before reshelving, clerks should apply two dots to the spine of each volume used which was not previously dotted.

Step 3: After one year, the clerks should tabulate and compute the dotted and non-dotted statistical data for 100 consecutive volumes which are being reshelved. This is the major difference between this procedure and previous procedures.

Step 4: Follow Steps 5 through 13 for books circulating (pp. 129-133). For this purpose, the word "circulation" means "use in the library."

The Procedure for Weeding Books Which Do Not Circulate, Used by the Staff in the Library

There are two conditions likely to be found for in-library use by the staff. If the books used are accessible to the clients as well as the staff, the staff-user should not reshelve these books. They should be reshelved and spine-marked by the clerks. Then all procedures in "The Procedure for Weeding Books Which Do Not Circulate, but Are Used by Clients in the Library" above are followed.

If such books are not available to the clients but are special collections accessible to the staff only, the following techniques are applicable:

Modification 1: The member of the staff using a volume must spine-mark it before it is reshelved.

Modification 2: After one year, the recording, tabulating, and computing of the data must be done by the staff users. This process becomes more complicated if more than one staff member uses one special collection. The recording of the data from the volumes being reshelved, as to whether or not they were previously dotted, must be done for 100 consecutive uses and later for 400 such uses, and might involve a number of staff members. A system should be created to ensure completeness of such recording.

Modification 3: In reference collections, use 98 percent or 99 percent as the cut-point, instead of the lower percentages recommended for other types of collections.

Then follow Steps 5 through 13 for books circulating (pp. 129-133).

THE SUBSTITUTE SPINE-MARKING METHOD

In several special cases it is not necessary to put a mark on the spine since some other mark is already being applied to the book. This substitute mark can be used as if it were a spine mark. Two cases of this have come to our attention.

The first is where the machine-charging method of circulation control applies a small colored dot on the back of the book card when a volume is being charged out. If this has been done for only a year or two, use the methods above, substituting the dot on the back of the card for the dot on the spine. Tabulate this information exactly the same way you would have tabulated a spine mark.

Another case found in the field occurred where the books were being stamped at the circulation desk with a legal warning that penalties would be imposed for not returning them. This was being done on a continuing basis and had been going on for over one year. This stamping is a satisfactory substitute for the marks on the spine, and the data should be tabulated as above, substituting the printed warning for the spine mark.

THE METHOD UTILIZED

Appendix B consists of an article by Marian Poller, reporting her experiences in using the Spine-Marking Method of weeding.

12

METHOD 3:
THE HISTORICAL RECONSTRUCTION METHOD

WHEN TO USE IT

This method can be used only where the book card method of circulation control is in effect, with the year of each circulation indicated. Since this also is true for the Book Card Method of weeding, the Historical Reconstruction Method can be used in place of the Book Card Method. However, the Book Card Method and the Spine-Marking Method are preferred for at least 99 percent of libraries. Yet, there are two situations in which the Historical Reconstruction Method becomes the preferred method.

Situation 1: The two previous methods of weeding are applicable when the library can observe and record the current use being made of its resources. However, there are cases when a major collection is used only as a feeder for local libraries. The use occurs at some distance from the main collection, and the central staff doing the weeding does not have ready access to current use records.

An example of a feeder library is the Bruce County Public Library in Port Elgin, Ontario. It is a central distribution library whose primary function is to stock branch libraries; the central library has no circulation of its own independent of the branches. The Bruce Library purchases books and distributes them to 21 branches and two deposit stations. Selected books are exchanged by the branches three or four times a year. In this situation, the Historical Reconstruction Method is the best one available to determine candidates for weeding.

Situation 2: Another situation exists where libraries are very small or have very little activity in the class of books to be weeded. The number of circulations per day may be so few that a sample of 400 might take months or even years to accumulate. For example, if in a pre-selected class of books only 2 circulations occur per day, it would take 200 days to get a sample of 400, and weeding would be delayed.

ADVANTAGES OF THE METHOD

1. **The Historical Reconstruction Method might save time.** In the case of very small circulation activity, no waiting time is required to accumulate 400 uses.

2. **In some cases, it is the only practical method available.** This is true for feeder libraries whose only clients are other libraries.

3. **It is a very complete method.** The book cards, theoretically, contain the entire use history of the volumes held by the library, and this is what is being sampled. While the Book Card Method of weeding studies only a relatively few days of circulation to predict future use, this method looks at the entire history of past use, or at least the last 10 years of such use.

STEPS TO BE TAKEN BEFORE WEEDING

Step 1: Appoint a weeding manager. Since this entire operation should take only a few days, a senior staff member should be permitted to spend full time organizing and supervising the operation.

Step 2: Organize the entire operation. A complete plan should be created, in writing, covering the following tasks:

A. Establish the date or dates that the actual weeding will take place.

B. Schedule the staff or volunteers who will do the work. A group of 10 assistants is sufficient for most medium-sized libraries.

C. Acquire an adequate number of storage boxes to hold the volumes removed from the stacks. Try to estimate the number needed, figuring that between 10 and 30 percent of the volumes are likely to be removed.

D. Acquire tape or string to secure the packed boxes and marking pencils to note their content.

E. If possible, get one book truck for each worker so that there is a convenient place to put the books as they are removed from the shelves.

F. Schedule a person to physically move the books or boxes from the stack area to storage areas. Maintenance personnel can be used for this purpose.

G. Locate and prepare adequate storage space to hold the books removed from the shelves.

H. Have a half-hour training session with all involved personnel before the weeding starts. (See Instructions for Weeding, which follow.)

I. Announce and publicize the fact that the library will be closed during the weeding period.

J. Schedule a day before the actual weeding for data collection and cut-point determination.

K. Get 3x5-inch cards, two for each shelf involved in the weeding.

L. Get foot stools, tall stools, and short stools so weeders can work sitting down.

Step 3: Test out the system in a trial run. At least one week before the actual weeding, the weeding manager should make a trial run both to create the cut-point and to identify candidates for weeding. This should work out any kinks or doubts in advance.

TRAINING THE WEEDING STAFF

As advised above, a training session should be set up in advance of the actual weeding. It is good practice to have this session immediately prior to the start of weeding. Here is an example of some weeding instructions the author has used several times:

Instructions for Weeding

1. Weed in a fixed order, from top to bottom and from left to right.
2. Place a 3x5-inch card in the middle of a weeded shelf, between two books, clearly visible, to identify that shelf as having been weeded. This is done so that no shelf goes unweeded or none is weeded more than once.
3. The cut-date is _____. (Insert the cut-date determined for your library.) Keep all volumes on the shelf which have been used once or more in _____. (List your cut-date first, then list subsequent years up to the current year. For example, suppose your cut-date is February 26, 1978. Fill in the space above: "Keep all volumes on the shelf which have been used once or more since Feburary 27, 1978, including all of 1979, 1980, 1981." The current year should be the last in the sequence.) Place on the book truck all volumes *last used* on the cut-date or earlier.
4. Many cards have the due dates appearing out of chronological order. Search out the date reflecting the most recent use as the criterion for either leaving a book on the shelf or putting it on the book truck. If a Gaylord charging machine is being used, look at all four possible positions to find the most recent date.
5. If a quick glance at a card indicates any date listed in 3, above (1979, 1980, or 1981 in the example), the book is to remain on the shelf. In that case, it is not necessary to search out the most recent date on the book card.
6. If there is any doubt about whether a book should be retained or removed, keep that volume on the shelf.
7. If a book has no due date appearing on the book card, keep that volume if it seems to be a relatively new book or a book that has been given a new book card in the last five years. Remove books from the shelf if dusty, yellowed with age, or containing old-style book cards.
8. Treat duplicate titles as separate works. This means that one copy might be retained and another weeded out.
9. Keep local authors, gift books, or special books of local subjects if you happen to recognize them. Do not worry about discarding valuable works since the weeding manager will look at each book before it is discarded.
10. Do not make a subjective judgment about keeping a book because you think the author, subject, or title is important. If the book card indicates it should be removed, remove it. Do not do subjective weeding!
11. If you have any serious questions, ask the weeding supervisor.
12. Work as comfortably as possible. The use of different size stools will cut fatigue and increase productivity.

13. Your early selections will be double-checked by the weeding manager, who will give you any additional training you may need.

14. If for any reason you are interrupted in the middle of a shelf, turn the last book observed on its spine so that you can start from where you left off.

THE METHOD SUMMARIZED

This method consists of collecting a meaningful sample of the book cards representing the entire circulating collection. Both the books on the shelves in the library and the books currently circulating outside the library are to be represented in this sample. The number of uses experienced over the last 10 years is then tabulated. This data is converted into shelf-time periods which have transpired between successive uses. The shelf-time periods, which describe the circulation pattern, are tabulated and a cut-point for weeding is created. Then the book card of every volume not in circulation is examined, and those volumes which have not been used since the cut-date established become candidates for weeding.

In theory, the Historical Reconstruction Method is based upon the concept that when book cards are date-stamped they contain the entire use history of the library. One weakness of the theory is that the collection is not intact: books and book cards have been lost, stolen, and weeded out. Therefore, just a part of the circulation record is available. To compensate for this weakness, the method concentrates on a recent time period. Instead of observing the entire use history, our method limits itself to usage during the last 10 years.

THE METHOD ILLUSTRATED

Steps 1 through 6 describe a method for undertaking "systematic sampling." This method consists of using every n^{th} book (say, every 200th book) as a sample. This technique assures sampling of all classes and locations proportionately. While attempting this method in Larchmont the aim was to tabulate 400 uses. It resulted in only 370 useful samples. This suggests that an attempt should be made to collect 500 useful samples instead of 400, as described below in Step 2.

Step 1: Estimate the number of volumes in the circulating collection. In order to estimate the size of the circulating collection, count or estimate the number of book cards at the circulation stations representing books currently circulating. (This, of course, does not apply to feeder libraries, which disregard volumes now controlled by the branches.) To the circulating volumes add the number of volumes currently in the library: on the shelves, being reshelved, or awaiting reshelving.

To prevent a confusion of terms, the "circulating collection" refers to all books permitted to circulate. The "circulating volumes" refer to that part of the circulating collection now actually out of the library in the hands of the clients, i.e., volumes currently in circulation.

To estimate the number of volumes on the shelves, count the number of volumes on 10 shelves, divide the total by 10, and use this number as the average number of volumes on each shelf of the library. Then multiply the average number of volumes on each shelf by the number of shelves containing the collection to be weeded.

For example, the following number of books were found on 10 shelves, selected as average shelves: 21, 32, 29, 18, 30, 30, 22, 27, 34, 27. This totals 270. This number was divided by 10, so it was determined that the average shelf contained 27 volumes. There were 1,170 shelves containing the circulating collection in this library. This indicated approximately 31,600 books on the shelves.

It was found that when book cards were packed tight, there were 80 cards per inch. There were 100 inches of book cards representing the books circulating. Therefore, there were 8,000 volumes in circulation. By actual count, 400 volumes were being shelved or located at pre-shelving holding locations.

The total holdings of the circulating collection were:

On the shelves	31,600
In circulation	8,000
Being reshelved	400
TOTAL	40,000

The Larchmont, New York, Public Library had approximately 40,000 volumes in the circulating collection.

Step 2: Determine the size of the sample required. As in the other methods, 400 samples are used for computation purposes. Since in this procedure each sample represents one use, and not one volume, a check was made of the book cards. Ten book cards were selected, and a count of the number of uses per volume during the last 10 years was made. In Larchmont, these sample book cards indicated an average of eight such uses. It was decided to take a sample of 50 volumes from this collection in order to get 400 samples of book use.

Step 3: Determine the number of volumes, separating sample volumes required for a systematic sampling. In Larchmont, the 40,000 volumes were divided by the number of samples desired (50). The resultant total was 800. In order to get 50 sample volumes evenly distributed throughout the collection, every 800th volume was selected from the collection.

Step 4: Determine the order in which the library will be sampled. A predetermined order should be established for the books on the shelves, the book cards of the books now circulating, and the books about to be reshelved. For example, the books on the shelves were to be sampled first, from top to bottom, from left to right, and the individual stacks were designated as to their successive order. Then the books being reshelved were to be counted in a predetermined order. Following these were the book cards for books circulating: by due date first, and then by call number.

Step 5: Select the first sample volume. Select at random any volume from the first 800 volumes on the shelves. In Larchmont, the seventeenth volume on the top shelf in the first stack was chosen. Remove this volume and place it on a book truck.

Step 6: Select the remainder of the sample. In Larchmont, an attempt was made to select every 800th book or book card in the circulating collection. The precise method of locating the sample volumes is to actually count out 800 volumes on the shelves or 800 book cards at circulation. Since precision was not deemed important, an estimate was made as to the approximate location of each successive sample volume. It was previously determined that there was an average of 27 volumes on each shelf. It was computed that the next sample was on shelf number 31, since 27 times 30 equals 810, and shelf number 31 is the thirtieth shelf after shelf number 1, the source of the first sample. To adjust for the extra 10 books in the 810, 10 was subtracted from sample number 17 used for the starting sample. The second sample was the seventh book on shelf number 31. Then volume 24 was taken from shelf number 60, volume number 14 from shelf number 90, etc.

For the book cards at the circulation desk, every 800th card was located by using a ruler to measure the thickness of the cards. It had been discovered previously that 80 cards measured one inch, therefore, 800 cards measured 10 inches. So a book card was selected by measuring successive 10-inch intervals and removing one card from each of those locations.

Each sample volume or book card was placed at a work desk. When the procedure was completed, 42 volumes and 10 book cards had been selected for the required sample.

Step 7: Tabulate the number of uses for each sample volume experienced in each year for the last 10 years. Use "Form: Step 7" below.

Form: Step 7

HISTORICAL RECONSTRUCTION METHOD

Form for Recording the Number of Uses in Each Year

Sample	Pre 72 Date	Year									
		72	73	74	75	76	77	78	79	80	81*
1											
2											
3											
4											
5											
6											
7											
8											
9											
10											
11											
12											
13											
14											
15											
16											
17											
18											
19											
20											

*The current year should appear in the last column, and earlier years in each successive column.

This is a mechanical task. Remove the book card from the first sample, and count the number of due dates for 1981. Enter this number in the line labelled "Sample 1" and in the column headed "81," as shown in "Form: Step 7-A."

Form: Step 7-A

HISTORICAL RECONSTRUCTION METHOD

Form for Recording the Number of Uses in Each Year

Sample	Pre 72 Date	Year									
		72	73	74	75	76	77	78	79	80	81
1											4
2											
3											
4											
5											
6											
7											
8											
9											
10											
11											
12											
13											
14											
15											
16											
17											
18											
19											
20											

This entry has been made from the book card reproduced on page 149. As can be seen, there were four 1981 dates, and the number "4" is entered on the form. Continue entering all of the relevant information from this book card relating to use within the last 10 years. In the example, there were four uses indicated for 1980; two in 1979; and seven in 1978. The form should now look like "Form: Step 7-B."

Book Card — Front   **Book Card — Back**

| VM   Cox, Albert W. |
| 480   Sonar and underwater |
| C64   sound |

DATE	ISSUED TO.
JAN 1 2 1978	
JAN 2 4 1978	
FEB 1 1978	
MAR 2 5 1978	
MAY 2 8 1978	
AUG 3 1978	
OCT 3 0 1978	
OCT 2 0 1979	
MAR 3 1980	
JUN 7 1980	
JUN 2 7 1980	

DATE	ISSUED TO
AUG 2 1979	
SEP 1 1980	
JAN 1 4 1981	
FEB 3 1981	
APR 2 0 1981	
JUL 5 1981	

HISTORICAL RECONSTRUCTION METHOD

Form for Recording the Number of Uses in Each Year

Sample	Pre 72 Date	72	73	74	75	76	77	78	79	80	81
1								7	2	4	4
2											
3											
4											
5											
6											
7											
8											
9											
10											
11											
12											
13											
14											
15											
16											
17											
18											
19											
20											

When all the data has been recorded, reslip the book card and remove the sample book from the work area. Now take each successive book card in the sample (52 for Larchmont) and enter the data on the forms. In the column headed "Pre 72 Date," record from each card the most recent date which predates 1972. This gives a starting date so that the first shelf-time period can be computed.

The raw data tabulated for Larchmont appears on forms for Steps 7-C1, 7-C2, and 7-C3.

Form: Step 7-C1

HISTORICAL RECONSTRUCTION METHOD

Form for Recording the Number of Uses in Each Year

Sample	Pre 72 Date	Year 72	73	74	75	76	77	78	79	80	81
1				1							
2	71					1	1				
3		1			3		2		3		
4					1			1			
5						1	3		2		
6						3	2	6	4		
7							2	2	7		
8					1	4	2		3	3	
9					1	2	2	1	2		
10								3	1		
11					1						
12					1	2		1	3	5	2
13									1	1	
14						2	9	9	7	2	
15	71.						1	1	1	1	
16									2	2	
17									7	2	
18			1			1					
19			1			1		1			
20				1	1	3	1	1		1	

Form: Step 7-C2

HISTORICAL RECONSTRUCTION METHOD

Form for Recording the Number of Uses in Each Year

LARCHMONT 2/27/80

Sample	Pre 72 Date	72	73	74	75	76	77	78	79	80	81
					Year						
1	68							2			
2								12	3	1	
3							1				
4			1				1	2	1		
5				1							
6				1	3			1			
7					4	3	2	1	1	1	
8				1	1						
9		1						1	1		
10				1	1						
11				1		1	1	1	1		
12	no use indicated										
13	✔ ✔		✔								
14	✔ ✔		✔								
15					1	1	1	2			
16						1		1			
17				1	2			2			
18	No use										
19		1				1	3				
20			1		4				1		

Form: Step 7-C3

HISTORICAL RECONSTRUCTION METHOD

Form for Recording the Number of Uses in Each Year

FROM CIRCULATING VOLUMES

Sample	Pre 72 Date	72	73	74	75	76	77	78	79	80	81
1						7	5	5	7	2	
2					3	4	2	0	2	2	
3						4	3	6	2	2	
4							10	6	5	3	
5								16	6		
6										3	
7							1	2		1	
8						5	3	2	3	1	
9									11	3	
10								10	13	4	
11					1	2		4	5		
12						12	(VOLUME MISPLACED)		7		
13											
14											
15											
16											
17											
18											
19											
20											

Step 8: Convert the above data into shelf-time periods and tabulate. The converted data is tabulated on the following "Form: Step 8."

Form: Step 8

HISTORICAL RECONSTRUCTION METHOD

Summary Form for Recording the Number of Uses
by Shelf-Time Period

Under	Over	Summary of the Shelf-Time Periods			
Years	Years		Total #	%	Cum. %
1					
2	1				
3	2				
4	3				
5	4				
6	5				
7	6				
8	7				
9	8				
10	9				
11	10				
	11				
		Total			

This is the most difficult and critical step of the Historical Reconstruction Method of weeding. In order to simplify the computation of the shelf-time periods between successive uses, two rules have been created:

Rule 1: Assume that the use or uses recorded during a year occurred evenly distributed during that year. For example, if one use occurred, assume it happened on the 183rd day of the year; two uses occurred on the 122nd and 244th days; three uses on the 91st, 182nd, and 273rd days; etc. Normally, this detailed breakdown will not be needed, as the shelf-time periods become apparent without much computation.

Rule 2: Assume that books circulating on the same day of different years have the longest possible shelf-time period. Thus, if a book is used once in successive years, assume the shelf-time period to be "over one year."

Another point to note is that a shelf-time period requires a beginning and an end. This means that if only one use is indicated, that sample cannot be tabulated and so must be disregarded. It also means that the *first* use indicated on any book card cannot be tabulated.

The computation of the data now proceeds. For practice, start computing the entries for Larchmont made on "Form: Step 7-C1" (page 150) as follows:

1. Sample 1 has only one use in 1974, and it cannot be tabulated. Shelf-time periods need a beginning and an end.

2. Sample 2 had one use in 1971. The next use was in 1976. Applying rule 2, the shelf-time period should be entered as one use under six years but over five years. Enter as on "Form: Step 8-A."

Form: Step 8-A

HISTORICAL RECONSTRUCTION METHOD

Summary Form for Recording the Number of Uses
by Shelf-Time Period

Under	Over	Summary of the Shelf-Time Periods			
Years	Years		Total #	%	Cum. %
1					
2	1				
3	2				
4	3				
5	4				
6	5	/			
7	6				
8	7				
9	8				
10	9				
11	10				
	11				
		Total			

Sample 2 had one use in 1976 and one use in 1977. Applying rule 2, the shelf-time period is entered as over one year and under two years. "Form: Step 8-B" shows the entry.

Form: Step 8-B

HISTORICAL RECONSTRUCTION METHOD

Summary Form for Recording the Number of Uses
by Shelf-Time Period

Under	Over	Summary of the Shelf-Time Periods			
Years	Years		Total #	%	Cum. %
1					
2	1	*l*			
3	2				
4	3				
5	4				
6	5	*l*			
7	6				
8	7				
9	8				
10	9				
11	10				
	11				
		Total			

Sample 3's first use in 1972, on the 183rd day, is used only to establish the inception of a shelf-time period and cannot be tabulated. However, three uses occurred in 1975. The first on day 91, the second on day 183, and the third on day 273. The shelf-time period between day 183 in 1972 and day 91 in 1975 is under three years and over two years. The other two uses in 1975 are under one year. The first use in 1977 is over one year and under two; the second use, under one year. The first use in 1979 is over one year and under two. The next two uses are under one year. "Form: Step 8-C" (page 156) shows all the entries generated by the first three samples.

Form: Step 8-C

HISTORICAL RECONSTRUCTION METHOD

Summary Form for Recording the Number of Uses
by Shelf-Time Period

Under Years	Over Years	Summary of the Shelf-Time Periods	Total #	%	Cum. %
1		2, 1, 2			
2	1	|||			
3	2	|			
4	3				
5	4				
6	5	|			
7	6				
8	7				
9	8				
10	9				
11	10				
	11				
		Total			

This process is continued until all samples have been computed and tabulated. The entire tabulation for Larchmont is shown in "Form: Step 8-D." The only entry that was unusual was made for sample 12, on "Form: Step 7-C3" (page 152). Because the volume had been out of circulation for two years, 11 uses for 1976 were entered as having a shelf-time period of under one year; and six uses in 1979, as under one year. The seventh use in 1979 was not tabulated because of the special circumstance.

Step 8-D

HISTORICAL RECONSTRUCTION METHOD

Summary Form for Recording the Number of Uses
by Shelf-Time Period

Under	Over	Summary of the Shelf-Time Periods	Total #	%	Cum. %
Years	Years				
1		2, 1, 2, 3, 1, 14, 10, 4, 1, 5, 7, 3, 2, 10, 29, 3, 9, 4, 1, 15, 3, 3, 6, 2, 2, 1, 3, 3, 25, 11, 16, 23, 21, 2, 2, 13, 13, 26, 2, 8, 11, 6.			
2	1	ＨＨＴ ＨＨＴ ＨＨＴ ＨＨＴ ＨＨＴ ＩＩ			
3	2	ＨＨＴ ＩＩ			
4	3	ＩＩＩＩ			
5	4	ＩＩ			
6	5	Ｉ			
7	6	ＩＩ			
8	7				
9	8				
10	9	Ｉ			
11	10				
	11				
		Total			

Step 9: Total the number of uses tabulated for each shelf-time period. There were 326 uses under one year, 27 under two years, etc. These totals are entered in the column headed "Total #," as shown in "Form: Step 9," page 158.

Step 10: Add up the "Total #" column entries and enter the total number of shelf-time periods in the sample in the indicated location on the bottom of the page. The form with the number "370" entered in the total box now looks like "Form: Step 10," page 159. Note that while only 370 useful samples were tabulated, this is close enough to 400 so that it was not necessary to resample the collection.

Form: Step 9

HISTORICAL RECONSTRUCTION METHOD

Summary Form for Recording the Number of Uses
by Shelf-Time Period

Under	Over	Summary of the Shelf-Time Periods			
Years	Years		Total #	%	Cum. %
1		2, 1, 2, 3, 1, 14, 10, 4, 1, 5, 7, 3, 2, 10, 28, 3, 8, 4, 1, 15, 3, 3, 6, 2, 2, 1, 3, 3, 25, 11, 16, 23, 21, 2, 2, 13, 13, 26, 2, 8, 11, 6.	326		
2	1	╫╫ ╫╫ ╫╫ ╫╫ ╫╫ 11	27		
3	2	╫╫ 11	7		
4	3	1111	4		
5	4	11	2		
6	5	1	1		
7	6	11	2		
8	7				
9	8				
10	9	1	1		
11	10				
	11				
		Total			

Form: Step 10

HISTORICAL RECONSTRUCTION METHOD

Summary Form for Recording the Number of Uses
by Shelf-Time Period

Under	Over	Summary of the Shelf-Time Periods			
Years	Years		Total #	%	Cum. %
1		2, 1, 2, 3, 1, 14, 10, 4, 1, 5, 7, 3, 2, 10, 28, 3, 8, 4, 1, 15, 3, 3, 6, 2, 2, 1, 3, 3, 25, 11, 16, 23, 21, 2, 2, 13, 13, 26, 2, 8, 11, 6.	326		
2	1																								27		
3	2								7		
4	3						4		
5	4				2		
6	5			1		
7	6				2		
8	7					
9	8					
10	9			1		
11	10					
	11					
		Total	370		

Step 11: Compute the percentage of use represented by each shelf-time period, and enter the result in the column headed "%." This is done by dividing the total number of samples into the total number shown for each shelf-time period. First, 326 was divided by 370, giving 88 percent for the under one year shelf-time period. Then 27 was divided by 370, giving 7 percent, etc., until all shelf-time periods indicating some usage were tabulated. See "Form: Step 11," page 160.

Form: Step 11

HISTORICAL RECONSTRUCTION METHOD

Summary Form for Recording the Number of Uses
by Shelf-Time Period

Under	Over	Summary of the Shelf-Time Periods	Total #	%	Cum. %
Years	Years				
1		2, 1, 2, 3, 1, 14, 10, 4, 1, 5, 7, 3, 2, 10, 28, 3, 8, 4, 1, 15, 3, 3, 6, 2, 2, 1, 3, 3, 25, 11, 16, 23, 21, 2, 2, 13, 13, 26, 2, 8, 11, 6.	326	88	
2	1	ﬤﬤﬤ ﬤﬤﬤ ﬤﬤﬤ ﬤﬤﬤ ﬤﬤﬤ II	27	7	
3	2	ﬤﬤﬤ II	7	2	
4	3	IIII	4	1	
5	4	II	2	1	
6	5	I	1		
7	6'	II	2	1	
8	7				
9	8				
10	9	I	1		
11	10				
	11				
		Total	370		

Step 12: Compute the cumulative percent for each successive shelf-time period and enter the results in the last column. This may be done by adding together the percentages already appearing in the next to last column starting from the top, or percentages can be recomputed by adding each successive number of cases to the previous total and dividing by 370. In the latter case, add 326 to the 27 cases for under two years. This equals 353. Now divide this by 370, and enter the result (95 percent) in the last column. Now add 7 more cases to the 353, divide by 370, and enter 97 percent in the next row, etc. See "Form: Step 12."

Form: Step 12

HISTORICAL RECONSTRUCTION METHOD

Summary Form for Recording the Number of Uses
by Shelf-Time Period

Under	Over	Summary of the Shelf-Time Periods		Total #	%	Cum. %
Years	Years			Total #	%	Cum. %
1		2, 1, 2, 3, 1, 14, 10, 4, 1, 5, 7, 3, 2, 10, 28, 3, 8, 4, 1, 15, 3, 3, 6, 2, 2, 1, 3, 3, 25, 11, 16, 23, 21, 2, 2, 13, 13, 26, 2, 8, 11, 6.		326	88	88
2	1	~~卌~~ ~~卌~~ ~~卌~~ ~~卌~~ ~~卌~~ 11		27	7	95
3	2	~~卌~~ 11		7	2	97
4	3	1111		4	1	98
5	4	11		2	1	99
6	5	1		1		99
7	6	11		2	1	100
8	7					
9	8					
10	9	1		1		100
11	10					
	11					
			Total	370		

Step 13: Determine the keeping percentage to be used for weeding. This has been discussed on p. 113 for the Book Card Method of weeding. When the level has been determined, draw a line under the box containing this cumulative percentage level. If the 95 percent keeping level has been selected, draw a line as shown in "Form: Step 13," page 162. The form has now been completed.

Step 14: Determine the cut-date to be used for weeding. This shelf-time period (over two years) is found in the second column on the left, and is directly below the line drawn in Step 13. In Larchmont, the form indicates that all volumes used in the library during the last two years be retained.

To establish the cut-date, subtract these two years from the date the data was collected. In this case, the data was collected on 2/27/80. Therefore, the cut-point would be 2/27/78.

Form: Step 13

HISTORICAL RECONSTRUCTION METHOD

Summary Form for Recording the Number of Uses
by Shelf-Time Period

Under	Over	Summary of the Shelf-Time Periods			
Years	Years		Total #	%	Cum. %
1		2, 1, 2, 3, 1, 14, 10, 4, 1, 5, 7, 3, 2, 10, 28, 3, 8, 4, 1, 15, 3, 3, 6, 2, 2, 1, 3, 3, 25, 11, 16, 23, 21, 2, 2, 13, 13, 26, 2, 8, 11, 6.	326	88	88
2	1	‖‖‖‖ ‖‖‖‖ ‖‖‖‖ ‖‖‖‖ ‖‖‖‖ ‖‖	27	7	95
3	2	‖‖‖‖ ‖‖	7	2	97
4	3	‖‖‖‖	4	1	98
5	4	‖‖	2	1	99
6	5	‖	1		99
7	6	‖‖	2	1	100
8	7				
9	8				
10	9	‖	1		100
11	10				
	11				
		Total	370		

Step 15: In the circulating collection, examine the book card of every book on the shelves, and remove all volumes whose most recent due date is the cutpoint date or earlier. This is the actual weeding process. One book at a time is removed from the shelf, and the book card is examined. In Larchmont, if the most recent date appearing on the book card was 2/27/78 or more recent, the book was returned to the shelf; if it was 2/26/78 or earlier, the book was removed from the shelf and considered a candidate for weeding.

Step 16: Inspect all candidates for weeding and return to the shelves those volumes not to be weeded out. This is a professional job and should be done by the head librarian, the acquisitions librarian, or whomever else is respnsible for building the library collection and maintaining its integrity. Here, judgment is involved. It is axiomatic that the fewer books returned to the shelves, the better the collection will be.

WEEDING BY CLASS

To weed by class, the identical procedure above (Steps 1 through 16) is followed, except that the collection to be weeded is only one part of the total circulating collection. For practical purposes, when applying the above procedures, consider this part to be the whole collection. Four hundred samples of book use should be used to create the cut-point of the class to be weeded.

CORRECTING A DISTORTION

The Historical Reconstruction Method has been designed to collect the needed data from the entire circulating collection, including the volumes now circulating. In practice, occasionally, the method is being used where the book cards for books in circulation are not available to the weeder. A serious distortion is likely to be created when the sample is taken only from the books remaining in the library, since the most active books tend to be those in current circulation. This was observed in Larchmont, where a study was made of the books in circulation and the books on the shelves. The data from these two segments was computed separately and summarized in Table 8.

Table 8
% OF USE HAVING THIS CUMULATIVE SHELF-TIME PERIOD

Shelf-Time Period under:	Volumes on Shelves:	Volumes Currently Circulating	Volumes Circulating and on Shelves-Combined
1 year	81%	99%	88%
2 years	92%	100%	95%
3 years	95%		97%
4 years	97%		98%
5 years	98%		99%
7 years	99%		100%
10 years	100%		100%

The chart can be interpreted as follows: of the volumes on the shelves, 81 percent of the uses in the past had a shelf-time period of under one year; 92 percent, under two years; etc. Of the books now out in circulation, 99 percent of their uses had shelf-time periods of less than one year; 100 percent under two years.

Based upon this data, if Larchmont used only the data from the shelves and selected a two-year shelf-time period as the cut-point, it seems that it would retain 92 percent of the present usage when it actually would retain 95 percent of such usage. To compensate for this condition, when using data gathered only from the shelves, select a percentage cut-point somewhat lower than would have been normally selected (say 90 to 93 percent).

ESTIMATING CUT-POINTS

When a certain peredetermined cut-point percentage does not appear on the form in the last column (see Step 13), the cut-point can be estimated by interpolation. For example, if one wanted to weed at the 96 percent level in Larchmont, one would use two and one-half years as the shelf-time cut-point, the period half way between 95 and 97 percent, which do appear on the form.

METHODS TO IMPROVE FUTURE WEEDING

For libraries that intend to make continued use of the Historical Reconstruction Method, the following procedures should be followed:

1. All new books being processed should have an initial date stamped on the book card. This gives a starting date to assist in measuring the shelf-time period, and prevents the weeding of a new acquisition which hasn't had an adequate opportunity to circulate.

2. Whenever books are rebound and new book cards are inserted, the old book card should be stored in the book pocket along with the new card.

3. Whenever a book is weeded out of a collection, its book card should be saved for future use in reconstructing the use history of the library.

4. Whenever a book card is used up and a new card created, the old book card should be stored in the book pocket along with the new card. All old book cards should be retained in this way for at least 10 years.

5. When books are returned to the library after a long overdue period, the date of reshelving ought to be entered on the book card. This prevents a book which had no chance to circulate from being weeded prematurely.

6. When books have been held in the librarian's office or taken out of normal use by the staff, the date of shelving the book in publicly accessible areas should be entered on the book card.

7. When books in the circulating collection experience in-library use, they should be date-stamped before reshelving.

8. Due dates should be stamped on book cards in chronological order, instead of random order, so that date information can be tabulated more easily.

13

SOME PRACTICAL CONSIDERATIONS

BACKGROUND

A number of experiences in library weeding have produced information and procedures that can assist in improving the results obtained when applying the recommended methods of weeding. Some of this information can be used also as a standard for comparison, for planning purposes, and to increase confidence in your findings.

SHELF-READING

Shelf-reading is one of the oldest of conventional library routines. It involves returning the books on the shelves to their proper sequence. For all of the recommended weeding methods, decisions for weeding are based upon the use or non-use of a volume during a given period of time. Volumes which have not been used because they were misshelved distort the results. It is common practice in university libraries that students purposely misshelve books so that they will always be available to the only student who knows their improper secret location. It is imperative that shelf-reading be done for the entire library at least once every six months.

WEEDING THE CARD CATALOG

One major operation implied by all methods of weeding is the removal from the card catalog of the cards representing works which have been weeded from the collection. This is an arduous task, and there are no short-cuts. It is a more difficult task than placing the cards in the catalog in the first place, especially if the work was done carelessly or if the cards to be removed are to be found in the more confusing alphabetical areas.

One might reasonably question the importance of an accurate, up-to-date card catalog in a non-research library. On the face of it, such a catalog seems essential. If it weren't, why have librarians expended such great effort and expense on it? It is certainly considered to be the principal locating and retrieval tool in the library.

On the other hand, if the card catalog is to be accurate and up to date, all cards should represent materials available to the user. This is never true. Since libraries experience a great deal of theft (2 to 5 percent per year, on an average), the cards of the stolen books remain in the catalog and represent a major distortion. To a lesser extent, misfiled cards, and all libraries have them, frequently represent materials no longer in the collection.

The only way to have an ideal card catalog is by taking inventory of the collection regularly and removing the cards of works which are no longer a part of the collection. If a library has the resources, it might opt to try this approach. In practice, this is not a popular procedure.

However, at best the card catalog represents works in the collection, not works currently available. A recent study in a university library showed that only 40 percent of the requested books were available to the user at any one time. If the catalog is to help users satisfy their needs, it is already far off the target.

Until much more is known about the use, value, and cost of the card catalog, this author is not adverse to *leaving the cards representing weeded works in the catalog.* This would not be too dissimilar to certain union catalogs which over-represent every library in a system. In case a user requests a book not in the library, the library should obtain that book for the user. Bear in mind that the likelihood of weeded works being requested regularly and frequently is very slight, since such works are in the non-core collection, which by definition is that part of the collection enjoying very little use. These volumes are unlikely to be in demand. Before protesting the heresy of not keeping the card catalog up to date, remember that there are many libraries in the world with high usage, heavy circulation, and good collections that are *not cataloged.* The author has seen a very impressive example of such a public library in Oban, Scotland.

DUPLICATES TO BE CONSIDERED INDIVIDUALLY

From the point of view of the weeder, duplicate titles of different editions or duplicate copies of the same edition should be considered as if they were separate works. There are four reasons for this decision:

1. Such a decision simplifies weeding. It can be extremely difficult to treat multiple copies as one. For example, such volumes can be located in widely dispersed places and difficult to bring together. At the moment of weeding, they might be in circulation, on the shelf, being reshelved, in reserve, or in special displays. In addition, volumes located in different places are likely to experience different use patterns.

2. Even if multiple copies are found in one location, different use patterns might develop because of physical characteristics of the volume — whether or not it has a dust jacket, been rebound, is torn, etc. Such differences can cause the future use pattern to vary. Little is known of the causes of book use, so to assume that similar titles will experience similar usage is not justified.

3. On the face of it, it seems unusual to weed one copy of a book and retain an identical copy. However, as long as one copy remains in the collection, the library has changed very little compared with removing all copies of one title. If all copies are removed, it is because of lack of use. If all remain, it indicates steady use. If

only one copy is retained, it indicates relatively light use and that one copy will be adequate for the demands likely to be made on that title.

4. If the same title exists in different editions, it is not unusual for there to be heavy use of the newer editions and little or no use of the older editions. Certainly such older editions should be weeded out.

WEEDING THE COLLECTION AS AN ENTITY OR BY CLASS

No matter which weeding method is to be used, a decision must be made in advance whether to weed the collection as a whole, to weed one or more segments or classes, or to weed the entire collection by class. It is not uncommon to treat fiction and non-fiction as two distinct classes, with different cut-points and different shelf-time period characteristics. However, any other subdivision can be made. In the example shown on page 137, the classes have been separated into the Dewey hundreds, fiction, short stories, biographies, mysteries, and paperbacks. These divisions, or even much smaller divisions, can be used and should be predetermined by each library depending upon the precision desired and the objectives of the library. Libraries that are attempting to satisfy some of the recreational and informational needs of small communities should not consider weeding by minute classes. Serious research libraries should break down the classes to reflect differences in use patterns.

It was found that different classes of books tend to have different shelf-time periods and different patterns of usage. For instance, fiction generally had a shorter average shelf-time period than non-fiction; and such classes as religion and travel showed a great variation from each other, with religion almost always having much longer average shelf-time periods than travel. Even among travel books, Carribean travel books seem to have shorter shelf-time periods than South American travel books, European travel books shorter shelf-time periods than Asian travel books. Obviously, the supply of any class of books, the use being made of the library, and the type of user all affect shelf-time period.

All this means that if a library were weeded as an entity, a somewhat different collection of books would be weeded than if the same library were weeded by class. For instance, if weeded as an entity, a library might retain 96 percent of the total future usage. This might result in keeping 98 percent of the fiction usage, 90 percent of the travel usage, and only 80 percent of the usage of religious works. If each class were weeded separately, 96 percent of the usage of each class would be retained, but the shelf-time period cut-point would have to be developed for each class independently. This is an onerous task and is worth the effort only when some meaningful purpose might be served. Weed the largest classes that can be reasonably justified.

One reason that different classes have different shelf-time periods is illustrated in Chapter 8 (p. 81), which shows that collections might not contain volumes in proportion to their usage. When proportionately fewer volumes are held in a class, the shelf-time period shortens; when proportionately more volumes are held, the shelf-time period gets longer. If the library is weeded as one entity, the library holdings will be evened out so that each class will contain a number of volumes proportionate to that class's usage. In the case of Harrison, the adult fiction collection contained 24 percent of the library's volumes. Those volumes experienced 48 percent of the total library usage. To optimize the library's investment in books, more fiction should be acquired until the fiction holdings represent 48 percent of the total holdings. Even this percentage is probably on the low side, since as more fiction is purchased fiction use will increase. Nevertheless, weeding the collection as a whole and weeding by class are equally valid approaches.

HOW LONG DOES IT TAKE TO WEED?

Records have been kept on the actual time it takes to create a cut-point and to weed a library. Each method has its own problems, and there are substantial individual differences between libraries. In addition, individual work output varies greatly.

I. **For the Book Card Method and the Historical Reconstruction Method**

   A. *To accumulate the basic information:*
   The time needed to accumulate the 400-500 book cards used to create the cut-point in the Book Card Method of weeding has been from one to seven days. While no substantial effort is required, the time is needed to permit 400-500 books to be charged out at the circulation stations. The Historical Reconstruction Method of weeding takes about one to two hours to remove the volumes from the shelves, tabulate the data from their book cards, reslip and reshelve the volumes.

   B. *To compute the cut-point:*
   The time needed to compute the cut-points in both methods is under one hour.

   C. *To weed the library:*
   The time needed to do the actual weeding varied considerably. Each book must be removed from the shelf, and the book card must be scrutinized carefully to see if the last date entered indicates a core collection book or one to be weeded. Careful records were kept in several recent weedings.
   Public Library A: A collection of 17,175 volumes was weeded in 3 hours and 15 minutes by the equivalent of nine and one-half workers, all experienced employees of this library. Removed from the shelves were 1,980 fiction volumes (13.5 percent of the collection) and 648 biographies (26 percent of the collection). The average worker handled 554 volumes per hour. These employees were working on their day off and wasted little time. In addition, it took five man hours to move the books and pack them into cardboard cartons (52 to a carton).
   School Library A: The collection consisted of approximately 10,000 volumes, of which 1,019 were removed from the shelves. It took 25 worker hours, each person (there were 11) handling 400 volumes per hour. This work was done by two regular staff

members, 10 volunteers, and the author. Putting the books into the storage area and into cartons took four worker hours.

School Library B: The collection of 9,000 in-library volumes was weeded by a group of inexperienced volunteers. They removed 2,965 volumes. They were slowed down by certain written entries on the book cards which confounded easy decision-making. The 10 volunteers handled an average of 200 volumes per hour, including the loading, moving, and boxing of the books.

It can be seen from the above data that a range of from 200 to 554 volumes were being handled per hour per worker. While this variability makes planning more difficult, it is good practice to weed a library in one day in order to minimize the disruption of the normal library service. This is possible since almost any number of workers can be accommodated when each works in a very restricted area.

II. For the Spine-Marking Method

A. *To accumulate the basic information:*

The time needed to receive the weeding signal is between one and five or more years. The total number of worker hours involved has not been recorded since such work was spread out over such a long time period and was performed as an auxiliary effort relating to the normal, routine circulation, processing, and shelving procedures.

B. *To compute the cut-points:*

The time needed to do the computation is about 10 minutes, if done with a calculating machine.

C. *To weed the library:*

The time required to remove 1,200 volumes of one class was under one hour, in one case. Most of this time was spent in moving the volumes to the storage area.

HOW DEEPLY SHALL WEEDING BE DONE?

One of the fears librarians have about weeding is that so much will be weeded that the library will look empty. Neither the clients nor the trustees are likely to accept this condition with pleasure. And in many cases the fear is a real one, especially when weeding is long overdue. For example, in one junior college library, 75 percent of the volumes had never been used. In this library, to weed at any level would have removed at least this 75 percent.

There are two practical solutions to this problem. First, if too many books are going to be weeded at the selected keeping level, increase this level to 98, 99, or even 100 percent. Second, if this higher keeping level still weeds too many volumes, return a percentage of the candidates for weeding to the shelves. Try to return those volumes with the most recent imprint dates.

Under normal conditions, weed out between 10 and 30 percent of a collection, depending upon the ready availability of shelf space or the need for additional space. A library can be weeded more deeply the next time around. In order to accomplish weeding at a level that retains 70 to 90 percent of the collection, estimate the likely amount of weeding by the following methods:

1. *Sampling the entire collection.* Apply the computed cut-point to a sample of 100 volumes, selected periodically from the collection. For example, if there are 100 stacks in the library, take the first volume in each stack and compute the percentage of volumes being weeded.

2. A simpler method is to *weed one stack* and compute the percentage of the collection being weeded. This method has the weakness that different sections of the library tend to contain different percentages of non-core volumes. However, as weeding progresses, adjustments can be made to correct over-weeding.

3. If the Spine-Marking Method is being used, it is easy to *see how much weeding will occur*, since all the unmarked volumes are to be removed.

CUT-POINTS FOUND IN LIBRARIES

The cut-points appearing in Table 9 are given in order that you may compare your results with the results obtained by others.

CUT-POINTS RELATED TO THE RATE
OF CIRCULATION PER VOLUME

A spread of cut-points from two months to over 30 years has been reported in Table 9. A further study into the likely cause of this diversity revealed an interesting phenomenon. The cut-point relates rather closely to the rate of the circulation of a collection, i.e., the relationship of the circulation to the size of the collection. This ratio is a useful predictor of the approximate length of the shelf-time period needed to weed. It was observed that large, highly specialized collections have much smaller usage per book than popular fiction collections in suburban public libraries. Table 10 illustrates the relationship. While it is obvious that these variables are not related one to one, a rough prediction of shelf-time period cut-point can be made at the 96 percent keeping level.

A SUGGESTION FOR THE FUTURE

For some years there has been a rather substantial swing away from the book card method of circulation control, especially in larger libraries. Some libraries are moving toward computer control systems; others are converting to the transaction card system, with some kind of photocopying of the essential data required. Both of these systems tend to destroy the usable record of library circulation, and they have made weeding unwieldy and difficult. It is suggested that manufacturers add to this intricate machinery a device that would automatically

Table 9
SHELF-TIME PERIOD CUT-POINTS AT THE 96%
KEEPING LEVEL

Library	Shelf-Time Period in Months	
Morristown Public – Fiction	2	months
Briarcliff Public – Fiction	6	months
Harrison Public – Fiction	9	months
Minot Public	12	months
Tarrytown Public – Fiction	17	months
Garland County Library	19	months
St. Laurent Public	24	months
Greenacres Elementary School	25	months
Newark Public – Fiction	25	months
Larchmont Public	29	months
Tech University	32	months
North York Board of Education	34	months
Trenton Public	36	months
Columbia Special	36	months
Fox Meadow Elementary School	39	months
Louisiana State Library	60	months
Deering University	60 +	months
Grand Rapids – Fiction	120	months
Cowles Special	252	months
Chemistry – University	324	months
Physics & Pharmacy – University	360 +	months

Table 10
SHELF-TIME PERIOD CUT-POINTS RELATED TO
RATE OF CIRCULATION

Library	Number of Circulations per Year per Volume	Shelf-Time Period Cut-Point at 96% Keeping Level
Trenton	1.4	36 months
Newark	1.5	25 months
Fox Meadow	1.6	39 months
Tarrytown – 1980	2.3	45 months
Larchmont	2.6	29 months
Tarrytown – 1969	2.8	17 months
Briarcliff	3.5	6 months
Harrison	5.0	9 months
Morristown	6.2	2 months

spine-mark every volume that is being circulated. It is further suggested that such a mark be color-coded so it could be changed at the end of each weeding cycle. The time has come when the importance of weeding be recognized by the manufacturers of library charging equipment.

APPENDIX A
FORMS USED FOR WEEDING*

BOOK CARD METHOD

Form for Computing Cut Date
from Circulation Sample

DATE	VOLUMES WITH THIS <u>PREVIOUS</u> DUE DATE	TOTAL #	%	CUM. %
1981**				
1980				
1979				
1978				
1977				
1976				
1975				
1974				
1973				
1972				
1971				
Pre 71				
	Total			

*The actual size of all forms is 8½x11 inches.
**Note: The current year should appear in the top row and earlier years in each successive row.

SPINE-MARKING METHOD

Form for Recording Whether Books are Dotted or
Undotted at Circulation Station

Class	Dotted	Total	Undotted	Total

SPINE-MARKING METHOD

Form for Recognizing Weeding Signal:
Summary of Current Circulation Patterns

Classification	Total Book Circulation	Total No. Dotted	Total No. Undotted	% Dotted
TOTAL				

HISTORICAL RECONSTRUCTION METHOD

Form for Recording the Number of Uses in Each Year

Sample	Pre 72 Date	Year									
		72	73	74	75	76	77	78	79	80	81*
1											
2											
3											
4											
5											
6											
7											
8											
9											
10											
11											
12											
13											
14											
15											
16											
17											
18											
19											
20											

*The current year should appear in the last column, and earlier years in each successive column.

HISTORICAL RECONSTRUCTION METHOD

Summary Form for Recording the Number of Uses
by Shelf-Time Period

Under Years	Over Years	Summary of the Shelf-Time Periods	Total #	%	Cum. %
1					
2	1				
3	2				
4	3				
5	4				
6	5				
7	6				
8	7				
9	8				
10	9				
11	10				
	11				
		Total			

A REPORT ON THE SPINE-MARKING
METHOD OF WEEDING

**Weeding Monographs in the
Harrison Public Library**   *by Marian Poller*

The Harrison Public Library serves a suburban New York community of 22,000 people, and consists of a main library and branch library. Recently, the time came when neither the main or branch library had any additional space available in which to expand their collections. The decision was made to begin a concerted weeding program at the main library, which in 1974 had holdings of approximately 35,000 volumes and a circulation of over 160,000 volumes per year.

The criteria for weeding were based on the shelf-time period of individual volumes—that is to say, the length of time during which a volume remains on the shelf unused by patrons. The goal was to establish a cutoff point so that all volumes which had not circulated for "X" period of time could be weeded, with only a minimal loss in predicted future circulation for the subject classifications that were to be weeded. The acceptable loss in future circulation was established at 4%. The rationale for this cutoff point, and detailed statistical analyses of this method, are more completely described in *Weeding Library Collections* by Stanley J. Slote (Libraries Unlimited, 1975). The weeding program at Harrison Public Library was carried out in consultation with the book's author as part of a testing program for the method.

Shelf-time periods can easily be measured if the book card system of circulation control is used. However Harrison Public Library, in using the transaction card system, does not record circulation data on the book card.

To solve this problem, a self-adhering red dot was attached to the spine of each book as it circulated. The dots were placed one inch from the bottom edge of the spine. Later is was decided to add a second red dot purely as a safety precaution in case the first dot accidentally fell off.

When the weeding program began, the clerks at the circulation desk found it quite taxing to adhere dots to all the books being circulated, in addition to performing all the normal routines required at that station. As time passed, however, fewer books needed

_____

Reprinted from: *The De-acquisitions Librarian*, Vol. 1, No. 1, Spring 1976.

NOTE: After part of the Harrison, New York, Public Library was weeded using the Spine-Marking Method, the library decided to continue spine-marking to assist in weeding the rest of the library. It is interesting that the weeder felt impelled to augment this method with some other techniques of her own. Such additions cannot be endorsed by this author.

dotting, and this function grew less laborious. It was later decided that the library assistants could efficiently dot the books when they *returned* from circulation, just before they were to be reshelved.

The Ninety-six Percent Core

A basic premise of this weeding method is that when 96% of the volumes of any subject class brought to the circulation desk for charge out are already dotted, the appropriately dotted books in the stacks represent a "core collection" which is satisfying 96% of the future circulation potential of that subject class. In the case of Harrison Public Library, the 96% that repeatedly circulated represented only a fraction of the total holdings in each subject class and was identified within approximately a year's time. The undotted books in the stacks were thus concurrently identified as prime candidates for weeding.

An important note is that *new* book acquisitions were automatically tagged with red dots during this entire weeding project. This precaution prevented them from being considered as part of the older collection being considered for de-acquisitioning. To prevent any confusion during later weeding projects, a different colored dot could be used as a color code.

Advantages of the Spine-Dot Method

The obvious advantage of the spine-dot method is that weeding can be done without opening volumes, since the criterion indicating noncore status (lack of a dot) was right on the spine.

A second advantage of this method is that a quick walk around the library stacks can immediately show which classes of books are heavily used and which are not. Given that the public library should satisfy the public's need, it is possible to identify easily those classes of books that deliver the greatest circulation potential. Specific classes will no doubt differ from library to library, but the generic advantage is so great, especially in days of tight budgets, that some libraries might consider dotting their circulating books for this reason alone. In a nutshell, where the dots cluster, so do the readers.

Additional Colors, Additional Tools, and Beginning to Weed

Although the 96% core was identified in approximately a year, the library's director felt that additional data should be collected to ensure accuracy. Therefore during a second year, blue dots were placed on the spine of the circulation books one inch from the top edge. During a third year, a yellow dot was added near the bottom edge of the spine. The ways in which this additional information were utilized will be described later.

Three other tools were used in addition to the dots in order to make weeding decisions safer. They were (*a*) the *Wilson Standard Catalog for Public Libraries*, 1958, 1959−1963; (*b*) the *Wilson Public Library Catalog*, 1968 and its supplements for 1969, 1970, 1971, and 1972; and (*c*) *Books in Print* (*BIP*).

In the Summer of 1973, weeding was started from the Dewey classes 000-799 and the biographies. It was decided that all books to be definitely retained would be repositioned so that the spine was horizontal (facing upwards). All books to be considered for discard would be left in their normal position. The clerk then went along the shelves and (*a*) *repositioned* any book listed in the Wilson catalog series (these would *not* be considered for discard) and (*b*) *repositioned* any books with dots of any color (these were part of the "core" and would not be considered for discard). The clerk *bypassed*, however, any book that was in extremely poor physical condition − whether it was dotted or undotted, in the

Wilson series or not. Thus the books left standing in normal position were all those in poor physical condition, undotted, or else not in the Wilson catalogs. These were to be the prime targets for weeding at this point.

Subjective Safety Precautions

Weeding is a difficult and delicate operation in any library, and subjective safety precautions should be taken. In this case, the library director felt that many of the books left standing might not have been given a sufficient chance to circulate since they were relatively new and, because the shelves may have been so jammed, it was difficult for the borrower to see books which were caught behind or shelved on top of other volumes. Recent books of a reference nature may not have circulated on this basis alone. Still other recent books were the only ones on a specific subject, such as a volume on making masks. It was decided to allow most books published from 1968 to 1969 to remain, even if undotted. Despite this decision, a great many books still remained for final weeding.

Further Checking

Still left standing were a great many books in poor physical condition (dotted and undotted), books that were undotted, and books not listed in the Wilson catalog series.

The books that were dotted (part of the core collection) but in poor physical condition were checked against replacement lists from the general library system to see if replacements could be obtained. They were also checked against *BIP* to see if new editions were available. Obviously, it was in the interest of the library and its users to obtain replacements (or newer editions) for damaged books that were part of the core collection. A great advantage of the spine-dot method, then, is identification of those books in greatest demand, but in poor shape—books which may have been inadvertently weeded just because of that.

Those books which were undotted but listed in the Wilson catalog series were checked against *BIP* for later editions. Only those that seemed to represent basic items were replaced or rebound, if in poor condition.

Weeding: Round II

The next round of weeding began in the Fall of 1975. This time a single title might have had as many as three different colored dots: a blue one on top and a yellow and red one on the bottom. A detailed check was made of those books from Dewey classes 327-330, including foreign policy, practical politics, and books on Congress and elections. There was a total of 330 books. Of these, 93 had no dots on them, meaning that they had not circulated in the past three years. There were 64 with red dots only—these had not circulated in the past two years. Those books with red dots only or no dots were examined and checked against the Wilson series (going only through 1972) and also against *BIP*.

From the no-dot group, 57 books were weeded. Thirty-six were retained. Ten of these 36 were kept because they were part of a series called *The U.S. in World Affairs* which was considered to have more reference than circulation value. Four of the 36 books were reclassified. For example, a book on Richard Nixon was reclassified and placed next to other books on Nixon, where it might have received more use in the first place. *BIP* listed eight titles as having come out in paperback, an indication of popularity. These 8 were kept, as were 16 listed in the Wilson catalog series. If these books did not circulate in the future, though, they would be prime candidates in the next cycle of weeding. It was found that the books with no dots were much easier to weed than those with red dots only, as these books were newer and might still be listed in future editions of the *Standard Catalog*. Half of the red dotted books were weeded. Of those kept, 2 were reclassified, 13 were listed in the wilson catalogs, and 11 were in *BIP* in paperback.

From examining this small group, the library weeder realized that buying books on foreign policy is no easy matter. Many of these books can become quickly outdated—how many books should be ordered on oil policies when any day there might be a complete decline in interest? There had been a decline in interest in such areas as Latin America and Europe, while the Middle East generated more circulation. Books on the New Left were found to be passé, and there was little interest in past political campaigns or in the House of Representatives. Similarly, books on the Republican and Democratic parties were shelf-sitters, while older books on U.S. foreign policy were no longer read, even if the originator of the policy was the author of the book. Books on the Vietnam War written before the war ended were also going unread.

Thus, the knowledge of reader interest gained from weeding was immensely useful in allocating the book budget. This brought up the old question of whether a library should give the public what is good for them, or what they want. If the library leans toward stocking books most in demand, a weeding program such as this will provide information on what is being read at a glance.

Weeding Monographic Collections and Circulation Increases

One interesting finding was that after weeding, circulation figures at Harrison Public Library jumped. The following is extracted from monthly circulation reports:

Relative Fiction Circulation (Percent of Total Circulation)	
August 1972—April 1973 (before weeding)	24.3%
May 1973—October 1973 (weeded May 1973)	51.5%
January 1975 (20 months after weeding)	54.5%
Absolute Fiction Circulation (Number of Fiction Volumes)	
1973 (before weeding)	38,890 volumes
1974 (after weeding)	47,107 volumes
Percent Increase in Fiction Circulation	21.2%

The fiction circulation per volume continues to climb; within the fiction category, areas like mysteries have even higher relative circulation. This has led to buying more mysteries both in hard cover and paperback. The same action is being considered for gothics.

Conclusions

It was concluded that the spine-dot method solved any remaining doubts about whether a book should be retained or discarded; just how far a library should go with dots remains an open question. If followed too strictly, a library might end up with a collection containing only mysteries, light fiction, books for class assignments, travel, sports, and cookbooks. Other areas getting heavy use were the 133s, diet books, craft, and art books. More books were purchased in these areas and they all circulated heavily. The ever troublesome question of the purpose and goals of the public library, then, comes immediately to the forefront when a weeding program is initiated.

It was also recognized that the Wilson catalog series has a number of weaknesses. Such lists are already somewhat out of date the moment they are published; they are also extremely selective, and include or omit works that might be popular with the library's clientele. The series represents, basically, librarians' selections, and theirs alone. They are also of little value when it comes to selecting material of local importance.

In conclusion, it is felt that the spine-dot weeding program at Harrison Public Library resulted in the retaining of books that are really being used and in leaving little dead material left on the shelves. This is especially true for the fiction collection, where weeding criteria were more stringent. A thorough, ongoing weeding program has kept the Harrison collection fresh looking, healthy, and vital.

Better Predictor. The criterion that will yield a core collection of fewer volumes that will still staisfy a given level of future use.

Classic. An older book that exhibits the same circulation pattern of new books.

Closed-End Shelf-Time. The time period between the last two uses of a volume.

Compact Storage. Various methods of storage that will accommodate more books in a given area than will a conventional stack arrangement.

Core Collection. Sub-set of the holdings that can be identified with reasonable assurance as being able to fulfill a certain predetermined percentage of the future demand on the present collection.

Current Circulation Method. The sampling of books as they circulate in order to determine use patterns. This is done by examining books or book cards at the circulation desk to obtain data. It assumes that current patterns of use at circulation are a valid sample of the total use pattern.

Cut-Off Period or Point. The exact time point that determines whether a book is in the core or the non-core collection; i.e., the criterion to be used for weeding. The most recent use date describing volumes to be weeded.

Cut-Point. Same as "cut-off period or point."

First Shelf-Time Period. Shelf-time period for a book before its first circulation; this can be determined only if the date of shelving is recorded.

Five Libraries Study. A 1969 research project undertaken by the author in five libraries: Briarcliff and Tarrytown, in New York, and Morristown, Trenton, and Newark, in New Jersey.

Harrison Study. A research project in which the theoretical findings of the *Five Libraries Study* were put to practical use in weeding the Harrison Public Library.

Historical Reconstruction Method. Ideally, this means reconstructing the entire usage history of each volume in a collection by using circulation dates on *all* book cards since acquisition.

Historical Reconstruction Method, Modified. Reconstructing history of usage over a shorter period of time.

Imprint Date. Age of a book as indicated by the most recent date printed on the title page or verso.

Keeping Level. The percentage of predicted use to be maintained after weeding.

Level of Future Use. Predicted percentage of use to be retained by the core collection; likelihood of future use of a work, based on its past use.

Non-Core Collection. Sub-set of the holdings identified as representing a very small amount of the likely future use of a collection.

Open-End Shelf-Time Period. The description of the characteristics of the whole collection; the time that has elapsed between the last use of the book and the date of the study. It measures the most recent length of time in which no use has been made of the volume.

Primary Collection Areas. Open stack areas, accessible to users, which house the regularly used collection.

Secondary Collection Areas. Storage areas less accessible than primary collection areas; normally not open to the user.

Shelf-Time Period. The length of time a book remains on the shelf between circulations. See also "open-end shelf-time period."

Spine Mark. Coded mark on the spine of a volume which indicates use.

Weeding. Removing the non-core collection from the primary collection area.

Weeding Signal. The first indication that the core collection has been identified, when using the Spine-Marking Method of creating weeding criteria.

BIBLIOGRAPHY

American Association of School Librarians and the Department of Audiovisual Instruction of the National Education Association. *Standards for School Media Programs.* Chicago: American Library Association, 1969.

American Library Association. Association of College and Research Libraries. "Guidelines for Establishing Junior College Libraries," *College and Research Libraries* XXIV (November 1963), pp. 501-505.

American Library Association. Association of College and Research Libraries. Committee on Standards. "Standards for College Libraries," *College and Research Libraries* XX (July 1959), pp. 274-80.

American Library Association. Association of Hospital and Institution Libraries. *Standards for Library Services in Health Care Institutions.* Chicago: American Library Association, 1970.

American Library Association. Association of School Librarians. *Standards for School Library Programs.* Chicago: American Library Association, 1960.

American Library Association. Public Libraries Division. Coordinating Committee on Revision of Public Library Standards. *Public Library Service: A Guide to Evaluation with Minimum Standards.* Chicago: American Library Association, 1956.

American Library Association. Public Library Association. Committee on Standards for Work with Young Adults in Public Libraries. *Young Adult Services in the Public Library.* Chicago: American Library Association, 1960.

American Library Association. Public Library Association. Standards Committee and Subcommittees. *Minimum Standards for Public Library Systems, 1966.* Chicago: American Library Association, 1967.

American Library Association. Public Library Association. Subcommittee on Standards for Children's Service. *Standards for Children's Service in Public Libraries.* Chicago: American Library Association, 1964.

American Library Association. Public Library Association. Subcommittee on Standards for Small Libraries. *Interim Standards for Small Public Libraries: Guidelines toward Achieving the Goals of Public Library Service.* Chicago: American Library Association, 1963.

American Library Association. Small Libraries Project. *Weeding the Small Library Collection.* (Supplement A to Small Libraries Project Pamphlet No. 5.) Chicago: American Library Association, 1962.

American Library Association. Survey and Standards Committee of the American Association of State Libraries. *Standards for Library Functions at the State Level*. Chicago: American Library Association, 1963.

Anderson, Polly G. "First Aids for the Ailing Adult Book Collection," *Bookmark* XXI (November 1961), pp. 47-49.

Ash, Lee. *Yale's Selective Book Retirement Program*. Hamden, CT: Archon Books, 1963.

Bedsole, Danny T. "Formulating a Weeding Policy for Books in a Special Library," *Special Libraries* XLIX (May-June 1958), pp. 205-209.

Berelson, Bernard. *The Library's Public*. New York: Columbia University Press, 1949.

Blasingame, Ralph, and others. *The Book Collections in the Public Libraries of the Pottsville Library District: A Date and Subject Distribution Study*. Pottsville, PA: Pottsville Free Public Library, 1967.

Boyer, Calvin J., and Nancy L. Eaton. *Book Selection Policies in American Libraries: An Anthology of Policies from College, Public and School Libraries*. Austin, TX: Armadillo Press, 1971.

Bradford, S. C. "Sources of Information on Specific Subjects," *Engineering* CXXXVII (January 26, 1934), pp. 85-86.

Branscomb, Harvie. *Teaching with Books: A Study of College Libraries*. Chicago: Association of American Colleges and American Library Association, 1940.

Buckland, M. K., and others. *Systems Analysis of a University Library*. Lancaster: University of Lancaster Library Occasional Papers No. 4, 1970.

Busha, Charles H., and Royal Purcell. "A Textural Approach for Promoting Rigorous Research in Librarianship," *Journal of Education for Librarianship* XIV (Summer 1973), pp. 3-15.

Carter, Mary Duncan, and Wallace John Bonk. *Building Library Collections*. 3rd ed. Metuchen, NJ: Scarecrow Press, 1969.

Cole, P. F. "Journal Usage Versus Age Journal," *Journal of Documentation* XIX (March 1963), pp. 1-11.

Collections Management, 1976— .

Cooper, Marianne. "Criteria for Weeding of Collections," *Library Resources and Technical Services* XII (Summer 1968), pp. 339-51.

Currie, Dorothy H. *How to Organize a Children's Library*. Dobbs Ferry, NY: Oceana Publications, 1965.

Davidson, Carter. "The Future of the College Library," *College and Research Libraries* IV (March 1943), pp. 115-19.

The De-acquisitions Librarian I (Spring 1976).

Donahue, Gilbert E. "The Library of the Cowles Commission for Research in Economics," *Illinois Libraries* XXXVII (March 1955), pp. 89-94.

Eliot, Charles William. "The Division of a Library into Books in Use, and Books Not in Use, with Different Storage Methods for the Two Classes of Books," *Library Journal* XXVII (July 1902), pp. 51-56.

Ellsworth, Ralph E. *The Economics of Book Storage in College and University Libraries.* Washington: Association of Research Libraries, 1969.

Fussler, Herman H., and Julian L. Simon. *Patterns in the Use of Books in Large Research Libraries.* Chicago: University of Chicago Press, 1969.

Galvin, Hoyt, and Barbara Asbury. "Public Library Building in 1973," *Library Journal* XCVIII (December 1, 1973), pp. 3517-23.

Gans, Herbert J. "The Public Library in Perspective," in *The Public Library and the City*, ed. by Ralph W. Conant. Cambridge, MA: M.I.T. Press, 1965.

Gosnell, Charles F. "Obsolescence of Books in College Libraries," *College and Research Libraries* V (March 1944), pp. 115-25.

Grieder, Elmer M. "The Effect of Book Storage on Circulation Service," *College and Research Libraries* XI (October 1950), pp. 274-76.

Houser, Lloyd J. *New Jersey Area Libraries: A Pilot Project toward the Evaluation of the Reference Collection.* New Brunswick, NJ: New Jersey Library Association, 1968.

Jain, A. K. "Sampling and Short-Period Usage in the Purdue Library," *College and Research Libraries* XXVII (May 1966), pp. 211-18.

Jain, Aridaman K., and others. "A Statistical Study of Book Use Supplemented with a Bibliography of Library Use Studies." Unpublished Ph.D. dissertation, Purdue University, 1967.

Katz, William A. *Introduction to Reference Work, Vol. II: Reference Services.* New York: McGraw-Hill, 1969.

Kent, Allen, and others. *Use of Library Materials: The University of Pittsburgh Study.* New York: Marcel Dekker, 1979.

Library Association. Hospital Libraries. *Recommended Standards for Libraries in Hospitals.* London: Library Association, 1965.

Lister, Winston Charles. "Least Cost Decision Rules for the Selection of Library Materials for Compact Storage." Unpublished Ph.D. dissertation, Purdue University, 1967.

McGaw, Howard F. "Policies and Practices in Discarding," *Library Trends* IV (January 1956), pp. 269-82.

Morse, Philip M. *Library Effectiveness: A Systems Approach.* Cambridge, MA: M.I.T. Press, 1968.

Mueller, Elizabeth. "Are New Books Read More Than Old Ones?," *Library Quarterly* XXXV (July 1965), pp. 166-72.

Mumford, L. Quincy. "Weeding Practices Vary," *Library Journal* LXXI (June 15, 1946), pp. 895-98.

Neufeld, John. "S-O-B Save Our Books," *RQ* VI (Fall 1966), pp. 25-28.

New York Library Association. Standards Committee and Sub-Committees of the Adult Services Section. Proposed Standards for Adult Services in Public Libraries in New York State. New York: Library Association, 1969.

Orne, Jerrold. "Academic Library Building in 1973," *Library Journal* XCVIII (December 1, 1973), pp. 3511-16.

Polson, Ruth E. "When Your Library Joins a System, What Can You Expect?," *Illinois Libraries* XLIX (January 1967), pp. 26-38.

Ranck, Samuel H. "The Problem of the Unused Book," *Library Journal* XXXVI (August 1911), pp. 428-29.

Richards, J. S. "Regional Discards of Public Libraries," *PNLA Quarterly* IX (1944), pp. 15-18.

Rider, Fremont. *Compact Book Storage.* New York: Hadham Press, 1949.

Rider, Fremont. *The Scholar and the Future of the Research Library.* New York: Hadham Press, 1944.

Ruef, Joseph A. "Fertile Fields for Weeding," *Library Journal* LXXXVI (March 15, 1961), p. 1112.

Silver, Edward A. "A quantitative Appraisal of the M.I.T. Science Library Mezzanine with an Application to the Problem of Limited Shelf Space." Unpublished term paper for M.I.T. graduate course 8:75, Operations Research, 1962.

Slote, Stanley J. "An Approach to Weeding Criteria for Newspaper Libraries," *American Documentation* XIX (April 1968), pp. 168-72.

Slote, Stanley James. "The Predictive Value of Past-Use Patterns of Adult Fiction in Public Libraries for Identifying Core Collections." Unpublished Ph.D. dissertation, Rutgers University, 1970. (University Microfilms, Inc., Ann Arbor, MI, No. 71-3104.)

Slote, Stanley James. *Weeding Library Collections.* Littleton, CO: Libraries Unlimited, 1975.

Special Libraries Association. "Objectives and Standards for Special Libraries," *Special Libraries* LV (December 1964), pp. 672-80.

Stieg, Lewis. "A Technique for Evaluating the College Library Book Collection," *Library Quarterly* XIII (January 1943), pp. 34-44.

Stoljarov, Ju. N. "Optimum Size of Public Library Stocks," *UNESCO Bulletin* XXVII (January-February 1973), pp. 22-28, 42.

Trueswell, Richard W. *Analysis of Library User Circulation Requirements.* Amherst: University of Massachusetts, 1968.

Trueswell, Richard W. "Determining the Optimal Number of Volumes for a Library's Core Collection," *Libri* XVI (1966), pp. 49-60.

Trueswell, Richard W. "A Quantitative Measure of User Circulation Requirements and Its Possible Effect on Stack Thinning and Multiple Copy Determination," *American Documentation* XVI (January 1965), pp. 20-25.

Trueswell, Richard William. "User Behavioral Patterns and Requirements and Their Effect on the Possible Applications of Data Processing Computer Techniques in a University Library." Unpublished Ph.D. dissertation, Northwestern University, 1964.

Trueswell, Richard W. "User Circulation Satisfaction vs. Size of Holdings at Three Academic Libraries," *College and Research Libraries* XXX (May 1969), pp. 204-213.

U.S. Department of Health, Education, and Welfare. *Survey of School Library Standards*, by Richard L. Darling. Circular No. 740. OE 15048. Washington, DC: Government Printing Office, 1964.

Urquhart, J. A., and Urquhart, N. C. *Relegation and Stock Control in Libraries.* Boston: Oriel Press, 1976.

Woods, Donald A. "Weeding the Library Should Be Continuous," *Library Journal* LXXVI (August 1951), pp. 1193-96.

INDEX

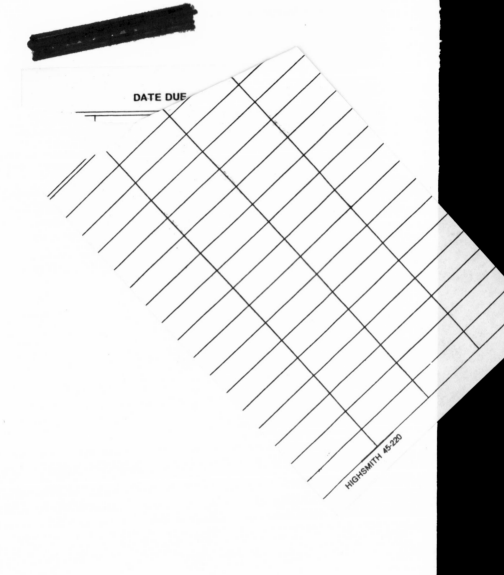

DATE DUE

HIGHSMITH 45-220

DA